YOU VISITED ME

YOU VISITED ME

Encouraging Spiritual Practice in a Secular World

Edited by
SANG TAEK LEE *and* ALAN GALT

Foreword by April MacNeill

WIPF *&* STOCK · Eugene, Oregon

YOU VISITED ME
Encouraging Spiritual Practice in a Secular World

Copyright © 2021 Wipf and Stock Publishers. All rights reserved. Except for brief quotations in critical publications or reviews, no part of this book may be reproduced in any manner without prior written permission from the publisher. Write: Permissions, Wipf and Stock Publishers, 199 W. 8th Ave., Suite 3, Eugene, OR 97401.

Wipf & Stock
An Imprint of Wipf and Stock Publishers
199 W. 8th Ave., Suite 3
Eugene, OR 97401

www.wipfandstock.com

PAPERBACK ISBN: 978-1-7252-9813-2
HARDCOVER ISBN: 978-1-7252-9814-9
EBOOK ISBN: 978-1-7252-9815-6

07/02/21

Scripture quotations, unless otherwise indicated, are taken from the Holy Bible, New International Version®, NIV®. Copyright ©1973, 1978, 1984, 2011 by Biblica, Inc.™ Used by permission of Zondervan. All rights reserved worldwide. www.zondervan.com. The "NIV" and "New International Version" are trademarks registered in the United States Patent and Trademark Office by Biblica, Inc.™

Dedicated to all those
committed to Clinical Pastoral Education in New South Wales,
as students, teachers, administrators, colleagues, and friends
over the past sixty years

Contents

Foreword by April MacNeill | ix
Acknowledgments | xi
Introduction | xiii

PART I: HISTORY, FRAMEWORK, AND THEOLOGY OF CLINICAL PASTORAL EDUCATION

1 CPE in New South Wales—Adapting to the Local Need | 3
   —Alan Galt

2 Clinical Pastoral Education: Bringing New Perspectives into Theological Education | 14
   —Peter Walker

3 Co-creation: A Model for Clinical Pastoral Education and Supervision | 26
   —Jennifer Washington

4 Prospecting for Grace in the Secular World of CPE | 39
   —R. Dean Drayton

PART II: CLINICAL PASTORAL EDUCATION AND SPIRITUAL PRACTICE IN A SECULAR WORLD

5 Black Fella CPE: Supervision in an Australian Indigenous Community | 57
   —Peter Powell

6 The Challenge of Supervising Evangelical Clinical Pastoral Education Trainees in Sydney, Australia | 69
   —Morris Sing Key

7   A Fallen and Upside-Down World | 79
    —Heather Robinson
8   "CPE Has Changed My Life!"—A Constant Student Refrain | 90
    —Rosemarie Say

PART III: ANTON THEOPHILUS BOISEN
         AND CLINICAL PASTORAL EDUCATION
         FROM AN APOCALYPTIC ASPECT

9   Apocalyptic Thinking, the Incarnational Jesus, and Clinical Pastoral Education in the Secular World: A Critical Perspective | 105
    —Sang Taek Lee

Notes on the Contributors | 135
Index | 137

Foreword

ALBERT EINSTEIN REMINDS US that "in the middle of difficulty lies opportunity," and 2020 has certainly provided many moments of difficulty. So much change in such a short period of time. In the midst of a global pandemic, life priorities have been reorganized as many within our community seek to "take stock" of their life. We find ourselves reflecting on the past in order to re-envision our future. As societies live in "lockdown" in order to survive, to minimise the spread of the Covid-19 virus, a deeper spiritual hunger has arisen. Confronted with the harsh reality of a soaring death rate as the world races for a cure, these experiences have provided the opportunity for many to consider who and what matters most in life, and what our sources of strength and hope are in a world that can suddenly appear uncertain, chaotic, and dark. It is in these places of isolation, uncertainty, and suffering where one could encounter pastoral care.

Identifying and responding to the spiritual needs of others is at the very heart of pastoral care. Informed by the insights offered by Jesus and the prophets of all faiths, and the humanities, pastoral care can provide a healing balm to another in a world that may feel broken. Yet stepping into this space of accompaniment, and seeking to provide a nurturing, sustaining, guiding, and healing presence for another is an enormous challenge. It demands that those who offer care have the intellectual, emotional, and spiritual resources to sustain them in their ministry. Fundamental to this process in formation is pastoral education and supervision. The role of clinical pastoral education is to help another build a solid foundation for their vocation.

As an organization NSWCCPE works collaboratively to "deliver quality education in pastoral care and supervision characterized by excellence in the development of pastoral carers, equipping for effective pastoral relationships, commitment to reflective learning, engagement of theological

Foreword

reflection on life experience, research in and ongoing dialogue on pastoral care and supervision." This mission is reflected in the writings that have been collated within this book, and highlights the uniqueness and talent that exist within our college community.

The editors of this book offer us the insights of specialists in the field of pastoral education. Combining the perspectives of pastors, pastoral care professionals, volunteers, and educators, this book provides the opportunity for many to learn from their experiences, and is a place where the words of Jesus in Matthew 25 come to life: "When I was sick, destitute, in prison, alienated, and oppressed, you were there with me." The chapters draw attention to the beneficial effects of the "action reflection" model of learning, for pastors as well as for the people they work with, and highlight the place of clinical pastoral education as the primary source of education and supervision in pastoral ministry in NSW over the past fifty years.

To the editors and writers of this book we say thank you for this valuable contribution to clinical pastoral education.

April MacNeill
President
NSW College of Clinical Pastoral Education

Acknowledgments

We would like to thank all those involved in the creation of this book: the nine authors who each contributed their chapter; those who wrote the endorsements; April MacNeill, president of the NSW College of CPE, for writing the foreword; Professor Emeritus Peter L. VanKatwyk, Wilfrid Laurier University, for providing permission to publish his diagram; Carolyn Craig-Emilsen and Moira Bryant, who read and commented on the manuscript; the researchers at Camden Theological Library for their guidance; Wipf and Stock for agreeing to publish this project, in particular, the editorial production manager, Matt Wimer, and editorial administrator, George Callihan; all our family, particularly our wives, Eunice Lee and Eleanor Galt, for their patience and understanding; Martin Kim, administrator of Iona Columba College, for his technical assistance; the CPE supervisors in NSW for their encouragement; and finally, all those who contributed to the advancement of CPE in NSW during the past sixty years. We hope this book will benefit all those who read and research about CPE.

Sang Taek Lee
Alan Galt
January, 2021

Introduction

IN MATTHEW 25, JESUS mentioned one quality that distinguishes those who are ready to enjoy heaven from those who are not, the capacity to offer loving care to those in desperate need of it: "When I was alienated and marginalized, in hospital, or in prison, you visited me."

In a world that prizes the opposite of what Jesus told us is the secret of faithful living, this book talks about how clinical pastoral education can develop the capacity for Christ-like love in people of all faiths, and none.

CHAPTER 1. CPE IN NEW SOUTH WALES—ADAPTING TO THE LOCAL NEED

This chapter traces the evolution of CPE in NSW from its beginnings fifty five years ago as a program for enhancing the pastoral awareness of theological students, to its current identity as the main ecumenical organization in NSW for education and supervision in pastoral ministry for people of all faiths. Alan's experience of CPE covers six decades: as a theological student; trainee CPE supervisor; supervisor; and supervisor trainer. He notes the way the CPE movement in NSW has adapted to the changing emphases: in the church; in the health, aged care, and corrective services systems; and in community attitudes, to retain its relevance, and loyalty to the example of Jesus, as well as Buddha, Moses, Mohammed, and the holy figures of all faith traditions.

Introduction

CHAPTER 2. CLINICAL PASTORAL EDUCATION: BRINGING NEW PERSPECTIVES INTO THEOLOGICAL EDUCATION

Professor Walker draws a parallel between the action reflection learning that is central to clinical pastoral education and the revolutionary approach of the fifteenth-century bishop Nicholas of Cusa. He describes how CPE enhances the personal, professional, and pastoral formation of theological students, which is a happy return to the early days of CPE in NSW when CPE was seen as an essential ingredient in the development of students' ministerial effectiveness.

Peter's own experience of being a student in a CPE program: "With the guidance of a wise supervisor, whose gentle exterior disguised a forensically perceptive mind, I visited patients, spoke with anxious families, sat with the dying, participated in bedside grief and then, in the peaceful meeting rooms of the hospital's chaplaincy department, discussed all of these experiences with the supervisor and eight fellow students . . . a valuable counterbalance to my preoccupation—book-based learning from academic documents."

CHAPTER 3. CO-CREATION: A MODEL FOR CLINICAL PASTORAL EDUCATION AND SUPERVISION

Adult learning theory encourages teachers to engage with the students in a mutual, collaborative process, recognizing the knowledge, skills, and experience of the adult learner. In this process, the teacher considers and is curious about how the students' prior experience offers insights into their new learning. In a clinical pastoral education program, pastoral supervision is offered by a more experienced practitioner to a beginner. This paper explores frameworks that have evolved to inform experienced practitioners' support for beginning supervisors and pastoral practitioners, by drawing from, integrating and building upon their prior learning experience. In this mutual, collaborative model knowledge is co-created.

Introduction

CHAPTER 4. PROSPECTING FOR GRACE IN THE SECULAR WORLD OF CPE

CPE prepares practitioners to visit and share with people who are going through times of emotional and spiritual distress, honoring clear secular boundaries as a basis on which to build helpful relationships, explore life purposes and, where appropriate, encourage spiritual practices. This paper describes a move beyond what is an implicit therapeutic model to a relationship grounded in the presence of God. Professor Drayton calls on a rich experience as practitioner, teacher, administrator and Church leader, to provide some challenging guidelines on how the ancient art of pastoral presence is more relevant than ever in a twenty-first-century world obsessed with the trivia of "success."

CHAPTER 5. BLACK FELLA CPE: SUPERVISION IN AN AUSTRALIAN INDIGENOUS COMMUNITY

Taking his motor home to outback NSW, Peter works with aboriginal elders to set up an effective training program for pastoral ministry which enhances and adds credibility to their pastoral visiting. This paper describes the joys and challenges he has found in developing a clinical pastoral education program within Indigenous Australian Christian communities, as well as in Pacific Island communities. Moving out of its Christian and Western focus, CPE has been challenged by different cultural views of providing care, the use of time and space, the meaning of stories, issues of power, gender relationships and identity, concepts of the divine, and financial considerations. Peter calls for a radical rethinking about conducting CPE, not just the programs themselves, but to allow the stories of other cultures to influence and change the way programs are run. This requires the dominant culture to give up social power in order to engage in a journey of curiosity with others.

CHAPTER 6. THE CHALLENGE OF SUPERVISING EVANGELICAL REFORMED CLINICAL PASTORAL EDUCATION TRAINEES

As a teacher of pastoral ministry, senior administrator in the NSW CPE movement, and primary provider of clinical pastoral education for Evangelical Christians over twenty years, Morris reflects on the challenges of supervising

Evangelical Reformed students, and the lessons learned. He describes four defining characteristics of Evangelical trainees: they are very wary and sometimes resistant to the process of CPE; their agenda or motivating need is to evangelize the patient (to "share the gospel"); they find themselves defending God, the church, and their understanding of theology against what they perceive as anti-Christian attacks; they have difficulty recognizing feelings and usually respond to pastoral concerns with thoughts and concepts. His recommended approach is to reinforce the students' commitment to Christ, while encouraging them to become more aware of the primacy of love and encouragement in Jesus's own life and work.

CHAPTER 7. A FALLEN AND UPSIDE-DOWN WORLD

On a follow-up visit after accompanying a woman, Louise, to an outpatient appointment at the eye clinic, Heather was stunned to hear the comment, "Wasn't that doctor awful! Did you see how close he came to me? It was like being raped." Heather remembered how the ophthalmologist leaned forward to examine Louise, his knees almost touching her knees. The lifelong impact of early childhood trauma and abuse on Louise required a sensitive response from a pastoral carer. What was happening here? How can pastoral care help in this situation? Where is God in the life of Louise and her ongoing sufferings? Clinical pastoral education (CPE) assists in understanding and responding to the deep concerns in people's lives, the everyday ups and downs and the more serious crises and abuses that occur too frequently in this world that sometimes appears to be upside down.

CHAPTER 8. "CPE HAS CHANGED MY LIFE!"—A CONSTANT STUDENT REFRAIN

Rosemarie relates this recurring feedback from students at the end of their Basic CPE program in mental health ministry to an exploration of their transformation from fragile, uncertain inquirers to people in possession of a plan for where to look for answers. She focuses on the uniqueness of CPE, which Anton J. Boisen, the founder of CPE, called "learning from the library of living human documents." Students are confronted with the reality of their own vulnerability, and come to see that wanting to know the answers is an impossible goal. Using anecdotes from her own experience of supervision and quotes from the pastoral care literature, Rosemarie

Introduction

illustrates how, using the CPE action/reflection model, students journey and grow by acknowledging their common humanity and coming to terms with their real selves. She has been uniquely prepared for this timely teaching role: as wife, mother and grandmother, daughter, sister, neighbor, and friend, she has experienced the range of griefs and losses associated with being a modern human being. Her clinical experience in grief counseling and family support, and in over twenty years in mental health ministry, have equipped her for her role as CPE educator in this specialized area.

CHAPTER 9. APOCALYPTIC THINKING, THE INCARNATIONAL JESUS, AND CLINICAL PASTORAL EDUCATION IN THE SECULAR WORLD: A CRITICAL PERSPECTIVE

Sang Taek Lee discusses what apocalyptic thinking and awareness of the incarnated Jesus in a secular society have in common with the approach of the founder of CPE, Anton Boisen. He shows how new hope can be brought to an oppressed and despairing society by a radical anticipation of a new future promoted by an enlightened pastoral approach to those overwhelmed by mental, physical, and spiritual crises in the real world we live in. Apocalyptic thinking is an open expression of the daily experiences of one's life and the Christian action arising from association with the incarnated Christ has a powerful effect on our response to the questions that arise in everyday life in a world that does not know Jesus.

Sang Taek believes that the practice of CPE is valuable to the individual, but it is also a social practice where it can be reflected on in terms of apocalyptic thinking, through examining Schweitzer's eschatological view in the works of Anton Boisen. He notes that we will see the opening of a new possibility of Boisen's living human document as a social biography when we act for the people with apocalyptic thinking, which is the presence of God that is already here. Sang Taek therefore points to the opportunity offered to pastoral practitioners, both ordained and lay, to bring the prophecy of Jesus that "greater things than I do you will do" (John 14:12) to fruition.

In these nine chapters, the contributors present a variety of perspectives and insights into clinical pastoral education, offering innovative ways to further develop the CPE model and to encourage spiritual practice in a secular world.

PART I

HISTORY, FRAMEWORK, AND THEOLOGY OF CLINICAL PASTORAL EDUCATION

1

CPE in New South Wales—Adapting to the Local Need

Alan Galt

EARLY DAYS: FILLING A GAP IN EDUCATION FOR PASTORAL MINISTRY

In 1960, lecturers at NSW theological colleges were looking for ways to offer effective training in pastoral care for their students.[1] On the basis of their experience of clinical pastoral education in the United States, they were supported by the Australian Council of Churches to form the NSW Council for Clinical Pastoral Education in 1963, to provide education and supervision for representatives of the churches who were offering pastoral and spiritual care with people who are experiencing health and similar crises.

Over the next thirty years, the Council for CPE expanded its activities and areas of interest to involve ministry in hospitals, psychiatric units, aged care facilities, and prisons, as well as in the community. In 2004, it changed

---

1. Rev. Dr. Geoff Peterson, videotaped interviews, 50th anniversary of CPE in NSW, 2013.

its name to the New South Wales College of Clinical Pastoral Education and became a member institute of the Sydney College of Divinity, to be able to offer students the opportunity to gain a higher education degree in the fields of chaplaincy and pastoral supervision.[2] After fifty-seven years, clinical pastoral education programs are still the standard by which other activities offering supervision in pastoral ministry are measured.[3]

ACCEPTING THE CHALLENGE

As hospital staff and administrators became more aware of the value of pastoral care in the therapeutic team,[4] they encouraged the appointment of chaplains and pastoral visitors, and in 1972 arranged for funding for a specific educational activity, clinical pastoral education, at the Royal North Shore Hospital, directed by chaplain Russell Fowler, that would prepare theological students and clergy for ministry with people in hospital.

At the same time, psychiatric hospital chaplains were experimenting with running training programs in mental health ministry at Goulburn and Gladesville Psychiatric Hospitals.[5] Mental health chaplains were also part of the move toward community-based treatment and rehabilitation aimed at reducing the increasingly expensive long-stay psychiatric hospitalization.[6]

It soon became evident that rather than spending all their time with the thousands of residents in the large state psychiatric hospitals, the chaplains' main role would be to equip the hundreds of local clergy and designated lay people from all churches who could lead their congregations into welcoming the residents leaving the long-stay wards for boarding houses, hostels, and sheltered accommodation in the community.[7]

At this point, the NSW Council for Clinical Pastoral Education began to offer formal programs of supervised training for church personnel, and started the process of educating and accrediting "supervisors" qualified to

---

2. Little, "Pastoral Enhancement."
3. Civil Chaplaincies Advisory Committee, *Role and Resourcing*.
4. Mrs. Kath Kline and Dr. John Yeo, videotaped interviews, 50th Anniversary of CPE in NSW, 2013.
5. Rev. Rob Hockley at Goulburn and Rev. Dr. Milt Coleman at Gladesville Hospital.
6. Rev. Eric Stevenson, Rev. Dr. George Stewart.
7. The "deinstitutionalization" move.

teach and support these people in the new and complex area of pastoral education in general hospital ministry[8] and in mental health ministry.[9]

WIDENING THE FOCUS

From the beginnings in the early 1970s at Royal North Shore Hospital, the number of venues offering clinical pastoral education courses expanded under the guidance of Keith Little: at St Vincent's in Darlinghurst, John Hunter in Newcastle and Westmead, and eventually Lottie Stewart, Carlingford, Gosford on the Central Coast, the Adventist Hospital, Wahroongah, and at Canberra in the ACT. Other CPE programs started at Goulburn and Gladesville Psychiatric Hospitals, at St George and Sutherland Hospitals, and with satellite programs for chaplains in Illawarra and South Coast Hospitals. Education in pastoral ministry remained focused on students coming from the NSW churches and theological colleges, and there was an impressive emphasis on interdenominational cooperation, with a common goal of helping people in hospital draw on their spiritual resources in times of medical and mental health crisis.

One CPE center opted to move out of supervision in hospital ministry to concentrate on preparing people for ministry with alienated and distressed people in the inner city.[10]

With the proliferation of church-run aged care facilities, a number of aged care chaplains were appointed, and church administrators as well as the chaplains themselves, began to look for opportunities for education in aged care ministry.[11]

The churches were also becoming aware of the huge population of alienated people in the state's prisons and juvenile justice facilities, and with the encouragement of the Department of Corrective Services, they began to place full-time chaplains in the large prisons and youth detention centers. Because in NSW we did not have any prison chaplains who were accredited as CPE supervisors, Corrective Services chaplains undertook their professional supervision with CPE supervisors who did not work in the prisons. This had limited success, as a credible CPE program assumes

---

8. Rev. Keith Little, Sr. Margaret Lee, Mrs. Diana Davidson, Rev. Dr. Barbara Howard, Rev. Dr. Les Underwood.

9. Rev. Dr. Milt Coleman, Rev. Alan Galt.

10. Sr. Evelyn Crotty, Urban Ministry Movement.

11. Rev. Dr. Les Underwood at Lottie Stewart Hospital.

that a student will receive supervision from a teacher who is familiar with their workplace and can help them improve their effectiveness there, by being aware of the daily challenges they face. We are hoping to recruit experienced prison chaplains to train as CPE supervisors to meet this demand, as happens in some other states.

One very effective contribution to professional pastoral education for prison chaplains has been their participation in Mental Health CPE Units, which equip them for relevant ministry with the high percentage of their inmates who have diagnosed mental illnesses.[12]

MINISTRY WITH PEOPLE FROM OTHER FAITHS

The population of NSW, especially in Sydney, is one of the most multicultural in the world, and with that comes a high percentage of our residents whose religious affiliation is other than Christian.[13] They have as great a need, and as much right, for appropriate pastoral care when they are in hospital, psychiatric units, prison, or aged care facilities, as do members of the Christian faith. The NSW CPE College accepts this, and has arranged for our supervisors to provide supervised pastoral education for people of all faiths (and none). This reflects the reality that the government supports ministry with people of other faiths.[14] Helping people from other faiths to have appropriate pastoral care in hospital and other crisis situations reflects the NSW CPE College's conviction that Jesus wants us to be available, as he was, to meet the spiritual needs of people who are not Christian.[15] Most NSW CPE supervisors welcome people of other faiths into their CPE programs,[16] but there have been CPE supervisors who have ceased their connection with the NSW CPE College because of their own denomination's opposition to our inclusiveness.

---

12. The 2019 Mental Health CPE Program at Macquarie Hospital, supervised by Mrs. Rosemarie Say, Mrs. Heather Robinson, and Rev. Graeme Watkins, had two prison chaplains as students.

13. Australian Census 2018.

14. The NSW Government under Premier Bob Carr allocated thirty-three subsidies worth $5 million per annum for hospital chaplains, including three from the Buddhist, Jewish, and Muslim traditions.

15. The Gospels have many stories of Jesus enjoying dialogue with people of different faith traditions: the woman at the well, the Syrophoenician mother; as well as the members of the mainstream Jewish religion, both his followers and his detractors.

16. The Mental Health CPE Centre Brochure, 2018.

At this time, some CPE supervisors accept only people of the Christian faith into their programs. Others offer CPE that is specifically designed for people from one of the non-Christian traditions, as well as running inclusive CPE for both Christian and non-Christian students.[17]

Several chaplains from other faiths—Hindu, Muslim, and Buddhist—are now training as CPE supervisors in NSW.

MINISTRY WITH PEOPLE FROM OTHER CULTURES

While most of our supervised ministry programs are available to people from all cultures and countries of origin, the NSW CPE College has agreed to provide specific supervised pastoral education for particular ethnic groups where that has seemed the most effective way of working: Pacific Islands and First Nations people;[18] Korean pastors.[19] Our supervisors have led Basic Units of CPE in other countries: Papua New Guinea;[20] Indonesia;[21] and distant parts of Australia such as the Northern Territory.[22] Of our thirty active CPE supervisors in NSW, eight are from Languages Other than English backgrounds: three Korean, one Indonesian, one German, one Finnish, one Maltese, one Turkish.

We are actively encouraging students from the wide range of ethnic backgrounds represented in the NSW community. In any NSW hospital, psychiatric unit, aged care facility, or prison there will be people who have come from all over the world, some as refugees, some the survivors of torture, many the victims of oppression by their own governments. The challenge for clinical pastoral education is to equip chaplains and pastoral visitors for the very sensitive task of being present for people whose experience of life has been very difficult, even traumatic.

17. The Mental Health CPE Centre since 2007.
18. Rev. Dr. Peter Powell.
19. Rev. Alan Galt, Mrs. Heather Robinson, Rev. Dr. Sang Taek Lee, Rev. Sarah (Moosoon) Kim.
20. Fr. Tom Ritchie.
21. Rev. Morris Key.
22. Jenny Washington.

Part I: History, Framework, and Theology

RESPONDING TO SOCIAL MOVEMENTS

CPE has always had an emphasis on identifying the sociological and cultural elements in a patient's situation.[23] Our supervisors have taken the lead in informing the churches on pastoral concerns ranging from abortion and euthanasia to climate change and renewable energy, and we help students be aware of issues as diverse as child abuse and domestic violence, to injustice and oppression of displaced minorities in our community.

By educating theological students, clergy, chaplains, and pastoral visitors in the importance of recognizing and responding to the many negative influences on individuals and families, the church and the community, we are helping to create a healthier community, as well as more fulfilled individuals.

In his seminal textbook on pastoral ministry, pastoral theologian Howard Clinebell called for

> an effective caring and counseling program, in which both minister and trained lay persons serve as enablers of healing and growth (which) can transform the interpersonal climate of a congregation, making the church a place where wholeness is nurtured in persons throughout the life cycle.[24]

This is exactly what the NSW CPE College has been working toward since we began in 1963.

THE UNIQUE CONTRIBUTION OF CLINICAL PASTORAL EDUCATION IN OUR ALIENATED WORLD

Whether they realize it or not, there is a spiritual dimension in everyone's life.[25] St. Augustine prayed, "Lord, you have made us for yourself, and our hearts are restless till they find their rest in you." There is, today, perhaps more than ever, a crying out for effective, appropriate, pastoral ministry that allows patients "to speak openly and with feeling about their illness, injury and hospitalization."[26]

---

23. NSW College of CPE, *Handbook*, "Standards for Supervisors."
24. Clinebell, *Basic Types*, 14.
25. See Johnson, *Pastoral Care in Palliative Care*.
26. McGregor, "Hospital Chaplaincy," 117.

The role of the hospital chaplain is very close to that of the dietician.[27] We provide nourishing and healthy spiritual food, and avoid the unhealthy and non-sustaining spiritual junk food that has often led to people abandoning the church, or perhaps worse, becoming pharisaical in their condemnation of people who they see as differing from their narrow interpretation of the Christian faith. It is appropriate that, like the dietician, we study and prepare ourselves for this task. That is where the systematic, soundly based, credible, and Christlike ministry of clinical pastoral education is so important.

The clinical pastoral education movement in NSW has adapted and updated the approach advocated by the founder of CPE, Anton Boisen,[28] to allow students to meet and get to know people going through the crisis of alienation from their spiritual supports, whether occasioned by illness, relationship problems, disruptive social and economic circumstances, the demands of work or vocation, oppressive family or community factors, or whatever causes or contributing factors in our modern world interferes with the harmonious development and continuation of their growth as human beings.

Our senior supervisors have researched and taught the essential elements of CPE[29] and as students have become more aware of what patients, inmates, residents, and parishioners really need in the way of spiritual accompaniment, they are more able to provide the pastoral resources that are appropriate to meet those needs.

This is a welcome contrast to much of what has sometimes been seen as "pastoral care" where church representatives have imposed unhelpful, irrelevant, and at times damaging demands on vulnerable patients and parishioners who are longing for the truly compassionate acceptance that Jesus offered to distressed people in his day.

CONFORMITY AND DIVERSITY

In response to a perceived drift to center independence, in 2017 the CPE College decided to make new regulations defining what supervisors and centers could do. Rather than leaving the management of their activities to center directors, the NSW CPE College found itself setting strict rules and

27. Church, "Healthy Diet," 67.
28. Boisen, *Exploration*, 185.
29. Howard, "Shifting Concepts."

regulations which all supervisors had to follow, not only in the important areas of ethical practice and proven educational practices, but in precise detail such as maximum number of students allowed in a program, required number of hours of professional development, and where to obtain professional supervision.[30]

The COVID-19 pandemic challenged the assumption that for "quality assurance" everything had to be done the same way. As a result of the "lockdown" of most facilities, and the strong expectation that all "nonessential" personnel, which was taken to mean most voluntary pastoral visitors, as distinct to chaplains, who continued to be welcomed and expected in most venues, CPE students were also unable to visit patients, residents, and inmates, or to meet face to face in CPE classes.

Our centers have responded in a sensible and flexible way, by adopting three different options: to cancel CPE programs until the visiting restrictions were lifted; to proceed with ward visiting, and face-to-face classes in those places where all safeguards were able to be followed; or to adapt the CPE program to the distance learning technologies that some were already using. So far the second option, taking students into the usual facilities where allowed, has not produced any negative responses, and the first option, postponing programs until a safe time, possibly next year, is working for some centers.[31]

We are evaluating the third option, meeting by Zoom, including practicing pastoral visiting in simulated interviews or with "guest" interviewees, comparing it with the "traditional" action/reflection method of learning from your own supervised face to face pastoral interactions, to see what has been lost, and possibly what has been gained, by using the internet technology.

Our supervisors are continuing their education in supervision online, rather than in the previously enjoyed live-in weekends that are no longer possible, with great cost and time savings! An obvious benefit has been the opportunity for supervisors from around NSW to meet more regularly, and to even invite guests from the other side of the world to lead supervision workshops, online.

I would be surprised if Zoom has not already become the preferred method for educational conferences.

30. NSW College of CPE, *Executive Minutes*, June 2020.
31. Report to Supervisors' Education Day, June 2020.

In October 2021, the International Council on Pastoral Care and Counseling will be holding a Regional Congress in Sydney, to which delegates from Asia and the Pacific are invited. It is highly likely that most of those attending, including speakers, will be online.

CONFRONTATION AND RESOLUTION

The NSW College of CPE, like any other institution, is no stranger to controversy. Over the fifty-seven years of our existence, we have had internal disagreements about policies and practices; opposition from external bodies questioning our theology because of our inclusive openness to people of other faiths being entitled to the same level of professional supervision and education as people from the Christian denominations; and our fair share of dissatisfaction from students who have had disagreement with their supervisors.

Mostly the difficulties have been resolved by our adherence to our aim of acting as Jesus would, and a comprehensive ethical procedures structure, that either prevents undesirable outcomes, or if they happen, provides a way to deal with them.

Our Grievance and Complaints Procedure Guidelines[32] defines specific ways of ensuring that a student's dissatisfaction is dealt with sensitively and with understanding, specifically by the college taking any grievance seriously, and if the concern cannot be resolved, by following a prescribed series of graduated steps to ensure that a formal complaint is dealt with fairly and effectively.

Where the set Grievance and Complaints Procedures have been followed, everyone concerned has been happy with the justice and fairness of the result and the sensitive handling of the problem.

THE FUTURE OF CLINICAL PASTORAL EDUCATION

Up to this time, the focus of CPE in NSW has been on ministry with people in health or similar crises, such as aging, grief and loss, and imprisonment, but we have accepted people for training in pastoral ministry from schools, university, military services, and police chaplaincy,[33] and we hope that the

---

32. NSW College of CPE, *Handbook*, "Code of Ethics."
33. Mental Health CPE Centre, *Annual Report*, 2018.

time will come when chaplains and pastoral practitioners from those areas qualify as CPE supervisors, and are able to offer CPE programs in their own workplace.

An outcome of the Royal Commission into Institutional Sexual Abuse was that all NSW churches, along with other institutions working with children and other vulnerable people, have been required to arrange for their staff to have "professional supervision." This task is far greater than the resources of the NSW CPE College can deal with, and we welcome the proliferation of self-accrediting associations of supervisors, but wait to see whether they deliver on their promise. A few of our supervisors have opted to join one or other of those associations, but most of us, seeing our role as not-for-profit-charities rather than business undertakings, have remained focused on our core task:

> To deliver Quality professional education in Pastoral ministry and Pastoral Supervision characterized by: excellence in the development of pastoral care practitioners; equipping chaplains, clergy, theological students, and pastoral visitors for effective pastoral relationships; commitment to reflective learning; engagement of theological reflection on life experience; research and ongoing dialogue on pastoral care and supervision.[34]

We are continuing to work toward creating an educational environment in which all chaplains in hospitals, psychiatric units, prisons, aged care facilities, and anywhere else that people are away from their homes and familiar sources of spiritual encouragement, are guided to fulfill the expectation that emerged in my research project forty years ago, that a chaplain

> is expected to be a listening, caring, familiar figure who gives comfort and encouragement in an unhurried way; is accepting, objective, trusted; helping patients work through grief; conveying reliability and reassurance, building confidence; motivating patients to rehabilitate; looking after the total person; giving spiritual comfort, discussing faith issues; showing interest in people's general well-being; helping people to understand themselves, helping people emotionally; aiding recovery by meeting spiritual needs; and helping patients to think seriously about their life situation. People expect in a Chaplain something of the presence of God.

---

34. NSW College of CPE, *Institutional Moderation Action Plan*, 2015.

This expectation above all other factors, is what distinguishes a chaplain from the other helping professionals.[35]

In line with our college's vision statement:

> The New South Wales College of Clinical Pastoral Education will be a leader in providing quality professional education in Pastoral ministry and Pastoral Supervision.[36]

This has been the story of CPE in NSW for the fifty-seven years of our history.

BIBLIOGRAPHY

Australian Bureau of Statistics. *Census of Population and Housing*. Canberra, 2016.
Boisen, Anton T. *The Exploration of the Inner World: A Study of Mental Disorder and Religious Experience*. New York: Harper, 1936.
Church, M. A. "Healthy Diet." In *A Dictionary of Pastoral Care*, edited by Alistair V. Campbell, 67. London: SPCK, 1990.
Civil Chaplaincies Advisory Committee. *The Role and Resourcing of Corrective Services NSW Chaplaincy*. February 2011.
Clinebell, Howard J. *Basic Types of Pastoral Care and Counseling*. Nashville: Abingdon, 1992.
Galt, Alan. "What Nurses, Patients and Chaplains Expect of a Chaplain in a General Hospital." MA Counselling Research Project, Macquarie University, 1980.
Howard, Barbara. "Shifting Concepts of 'the Living Human Document.'" NSW College of CPE, online, September 2017.
Johnson, Debbie. *Pastoral Care in Palliative Care*. Neringah Hospital, Wahroonga, NSW, 2015.
Little, Keith. "Pastoral Enhancement—a Short History of the New South Wales College of Clinical Pastoral Education." Master's thesis, Sydney College of Divinity, 2009.
McGregor, Thomas S. "Hospital Chaplaincy." In *A Dictionary of Pastoral Care*, edited by Alistair V. Campbell, 117–18. London: SPCK, 1990.
Mental Health CPE Centre. *CPE Programs*, 2019.
Mental Health CPE Centre. *Annual Report*, 2018.
NSW College of CPE. *Executive Minutes*, June 2020.
NSW College of CPE. *Handbook, Code of Ethics*, 2016.
NSW College of CPE. *Institutional Moderation Action Plan*, 2015.
NSW College of CPE. *Report to Supervisors' Education Day*, May 2020.
NSW College of CPE. *The Beginnings of CPE in NSW*. Video recordings of interviews with the pioneers of CPE in NSW, Geoff Peterson, Kath Kline, John Yeo, and Eric Stevenson, 2015.

---

35. Galt, "What Nurses, Patients and Chaplains Expect."
36. NSW College of CPE, *Institutional Moderation Action Plan*, 2015.

2

Clinical Pastoral Education
Bringing New Perspectives into Theological Education

Peter Walker

INTRODUCTION

I RECALL MY OWN introduction to the world of clinical pastoral education (CPE) quite clearly, now some twenty-five years afterward. I had been accepted as a candidate for ordained ministry in my mid-twenties and, according to the panel making that selection, I presented as someone whose formation for ministry would be enhanced if I were exposed to challenging field-based pastoral experiences. The college in which I was undertaking my theological education therefore sent me for a full year of CPE at one of Sydney's largest hospitals. With the guidance of a wise supervisor, whose gentle exterior disguised a forensically perceptive mind, I visited patients, spoke with anxious families, sat with the dying, participated in bedside grief and then, in the peaceful meeting rooms of the hospital's chaplaincy department, discussed all of these experiences with the supervisor and eight fellow students. The selectors who believed I needed this exposure were right. Those pastoral challenges were a valuable counterbalance to my preoccupation: book-based learning from academic documents. My college leaders were also right. A CPE unit offered the perfect way to achieve the sought-after broadening of my theological education: field-based learning from living human documents.[1] To put my experience in the following statement seems so obvious and, yet, the obvious needs stating to me then and is perhaps worth stating again today: I learned so much about the realities of life from my encounter with the reality of life.

Among the lasting legacies to me from that CPE experience is the priority I have sought to place ever since on reflecting with a group of colleagues on pastoral encounters, critical incidents, and prickly theological issues. Therefore, in this chapter, I will honour the significance of CPE by offering a fifteenth-century analogy for the value of that program and its case study method for learning from pastoral encounters. The analogy is in the form of an exercise offered by Nicholas of Cusa (1401–1464) to a group of monks for whom he was bishop in the German diocese of Brixen. Nicholas's exercise is one way to demonstrate the value of the method of case studies, in a group setting, that are focused on a critical pastoral incident. All who are familiar with CPE will be acquainted with the format: a clinical workshop, in which one member of a learning cohort describes and reflects on a challenging pastoral event from their field experience, and is then encouraged and nudged toward alternative and perhaps new perspectives on the incident by their fellow learners. We will come to Nicholas of Cusa shortly, however, we should first take a moment to mark the significance of the CPE movement over the last one hundred years in bridging the gap between theory and practice in preparing people for pastoral ministries.[2]

CPE AND THEOLOGICAL EDUCATION

The pendulum between theory and practice in theological education had begun leaning too heavily, particularly in Protestant faculties and colleges, toward theory; toward the academy. It was Friedrich Schleiermacher, in an effort to secure a place for theology in the modern university, who sought to cast theology as a science, comparing it with medicine and law. In that spirit, colleges and seminaries were producing minsters who were learned experts in the Bible and Christian tradition; the parish *scholar in residence*. It is a generalization, of course, yet not too great a stretch to observe that

---

1. Boisen, *Out of the Depths*, 187.
2. Anderson, "Integration," 13–14.

this saw an increasing gap between the minister and the everyday life of those to whom they were a pastor and preacher.[3] I was a typical example of the need to correct that balance: a candidate for ordination who needed experience in a chaplaincy setting to encourage the integration of academic theological study with ministry practice. Even though other traditions had their version of this gap between theory to practice, it is no surprise that CPE had its origins in the liberal Protestant tradition.

Thus, CPE took an important place in the world of theological education as a form of experience-based learning; a period of supervised practice of ministry, in designated pastoral settings, most frequently in hospitals where life can be so vulnerable. In fact, CPE developed, initially, from social service summer schools convened by a Christian physician in a Cincinnati hospital in 1923, an endeavour that sought to bring students preparing for ministry into direct contact with people in need of care—both medical and spiritual.

Anton Boisen later developed the most telling metaphor to guide the CPE movement and its method: the aim was to add real people, whom he called *living human documents*, to the other texts that theological students were already studying, namely, biblical, historical, and theological works.

> What was new was the approach. In a time when students of religions were making little use of the methods of science, and scientists were failing to carry their inquiries to the level of the religious, we were seeking to make empirical studies of living human documents, particularly those in which men (sic) were breaking or had broken under the stress of moral crisis. We were proposing to alter the basic structure of theological education.[4]

To observe and engage with a patient struggling with illness was every bit as important to theological education as was reading and engaging with the classic texts of a student's religious tradition.

By the mid-twentieth century, CPE began to draw intentionally on the findings and practices of modern medicine, psychotherapy, and the behavioral sciences. Thus, the value of close observation and the method of case study was added to the CPE experience. Mind you, medical and psychological models of care did not override the pastoral; they enhanced them.

---

3. Miller-McLemore, "Revisiting," 5–7.
4. Boisen, *Out of the Depths*, 187.

The method of case notes, then case study, and eventually verbatims or word-for-word transcriptions of pastoral interactions emerged as a pedagogical hallmark. The case, presented and discussed in the bounded context of a small group of peers with close oversight of a supervisor, provides a self-contained unit of practice available for analysis and reflection.[5]

Interestingly, it was recognized early that verbatims say as much about the observer as they do about the observed. That is, the verbatim is both a window into the mind of the one who is describing the pastoral incident to their fellow CPE students and a window onto the pastoral incident being reconstructed. Verbatims set within a case study method, namely, actual pastoral conversations shared in detail and then discussed within a small group of fellow learners, became a way to reveal previously unrecognized elements of one's own worldview. Those perspectives, fashioned by the settings of our life, deeply shape how we respond in any situation. Bringing those perceptions—those worldviews—to the level of self-awareness is vitally important in the formation of healthy pastoral identity and practice.

By the 1990s, broader developments in pastoral theology saw the metaphor of *living human document* challenged and enhanced by a new metaphor: the *living human web*. This marked a shift from "care narrowly defined as counselling to care understood as part of a wide cultural, social, and religious context."[6] The *human web* is a less restricting metaphor than the *human document*. It encourages the connection of relevant people and associations to the person in order to provide breadth to the understanding of her or his life situation and more meaningful pastoral care. Careful attention and support to the individual continued, of course. However, greater attention was given to recognizing each person as an individual set within a web of commitments and constraints; in other words, we are all woven into an occasionally complex web of relationships.

The key to the CPE program, and the driver for new understanding gained within it, were the regular sessions of group reflection. Whether the leading metaphor was the living human document or the living human web, learning from each other was central. And so it is at this point that we might turn to Nicholas of Cusa, and an exercise he developed to demonstrate the epistemological value of engaging different perspectives in our search for knowledge.

5. Miller-McLemore, "Revisiting," 8.
6. Miller-McLemore, "Living Human Web," 14.

Part I: History, Framework, and Theology

NICHOLAS OF CUSA

Nicholas of Cusa is not well known beyond a modest number of academics, a devoted group of *Cusa specialists*, and so a brief introduction to his life and writings may be helpful.

Nicholas was born in 1401 beside the Mosel River, upon which his father was a boatman. His powerful curiosity soon led Nicholas well beyond the life into which he was born. He studied liberal arts at the University of Heidelberg, graduated with a doctorate in canon law from the University of Padua, and studied theology and philosophy at the University of Cologne.[7] Nicholas was an eclectic thinker and so, alongside these formal studies, he developed an interest in art, architecture, mathematics, and philosophy.[8] He was among the first to speculate that the universe may be infinite and thus, given the impossibility of locating the center of that which is infinite, he also proposed that it was not possible to say with certainty that the earth is the center of the universe. He invented the concave lens, along with various instruments for measuring the level of moisture in the air, and the second oldest known map of Europe is thought to be the work of his hand.

Nicholas's brilliance was recognized early and, upon graduating in canon law, he was offered a professorship at the University of Leuven,[9] which he nevertheless declined in order to become an advisor to the Archbishop of Trier. From that post, he found himself a key player at the Council of Basel in the 1430s, an experience that provoked his first major writings, *De concordanta catholica* (The Catholic Concordance, 1433) and *De docta ignorantia* (On Learned Ignorance, 1440). Occupying a pivotal position in Nicholas's writings from Basel onward was the concept of *coincidentia oppositorum*—the coincidence of opposites.[10] His signature variation on that concept was to propose that the path to the knowledge of God reaches its destination only at *coincidentia oppositorum*, at the coincidence of opposites. This idea is emblematic of his quest for understanding and, in grasping this idea, we grasp much about the way Nicholas's mind worked.

The principles of reason call on us to distinguish between opposites. For example, a red light is not a green light, a circle is not a square, a liquid is not a solid, and so on. In this way, we delineate between one thing

---

7. Theruvathu, *Ineffabilis*, 3.
8. Meuthen, *Nicholas*, 15–21.
9. Theruvathu, *Ineffabilis*, 4.
10. Hopkins, *Nicholas*, 67.

and another in order to define it and, thereby, know what the thing is (and what it is not). To define is to make finite (de fine), a process in which we discriminate between one thing and another by comparing, contrasting, distinguishing, and, ultimately, defining the world around us. Yet Nicholas argued that this method of comparing and distinguishing in order to define breaks down in the course of any attempt to attain knowledge of that which cannot be made finite, that which we cannot define, namely, that which is infinite.[11]

Given it was fundamental to Nicholas's Christian faith that God is infinite,[12] he taught that knowledge of God is attained when we apprehend that God, who is beyond de-*fining*, is encountered only as we transcend this process of distinction and definition; only as we transcend the notion that knowledge of God can be achieved via a series of contradictions and oppositions. When the limitations of reason are recognized, and only then, we begin to perceive that the infinite God is ahead of us, at a place of mystery within which all rational distinctions coincide. In apprehending this path, which Nicholas likened to entering a cloud or mist, we begin to perceive a path to an understanding of God as the One in whom all oppositions are enfolded; the *coincidentia oppositorum*.[13]

For this style of epistemological wrestling with the knowledge of God, and his other contributions to the intellectual history of Europe, Nicholas has been described as Germany's finest fifteenth-century philosopher.[14] One of the most apposite descriptions of Nicholas was offered by George

---

11. We should note that Nicholas's idea is not that God is the coincidence of opposites. Rather, his proposal is that knowledge of God comes as we enter the darkness and the paradise of knowing that is encountered beyond the contradictories of reason; a paradise in which there is the coincidence of opposition. We should also note that this knowledge of God does indeed pass through reason. It does not neglect of reason. Yet, nonetheless, the knowledge of God transcends reason.

12. "The concept of *infinitas absoluta* is the primary perspective of all Cusanus' decisions attempting to express God's being as an absolute." Monaco, *Nicholas*, 121.

13. Here, where the mystery of God seems most impenetrable, at a place Nicholas describes as "beyond the wall of Paradise," we approach God. "Hence, I experience the necessity for me to enter into obscuring mist and to admit the coincidence of opposites, beyond all capacity of reason, and to seek truth where impossibility appears. And when—beyond that [rational capacity] and beyond every most lofty intellectual ascent as well—I come to that which is unknown to every intellect and which every intellect judges to be very far removed from the truth, there You are present, my God, You who are Absolute Necessity." Nicholas of Cusa, *De visione Dei* (1453), ch. 9, para. 38–39, trans. Jasper Hopkins, in *Nicholas of Cusa's Dialectical Mysticism*.

14. Duclow, "Life and Work," 26.

Sarton in his study of the early scientists of the Renaissance: "a Prince of the church but also a philosopher; a man of science with bold ideas, a forerunner of Erasmus."[15] Nicholas was made bishop and then cardinal in the 1450s, and concluded his ecclesial career as the vicar-general of Rome. He died in 1464.

Of special interest is the fact that Nicholas was among the first Christian thinkers to advocate for dialogue as a means of achieving peace among the religions. Within months of the fall of Constantinople in 1453, while Europe was mired in fear and showered with anti-Muslim polemic, he wrote *De pace fidei* (On the Peace of Faith, 1453) and, soon after, *De vision Dei* (On the Vision of God, 1453). Both books stood in irenic contrast to the prevailing mood of inter-religious suspicion. Michel de Certeau sets the scene by observing that, in 1453, the "world is coming apart":

> To the West, the Hundred Year's War (1337–1453) between France and England has ended. A period of nations is beginning. To the East, the Eastern Roman Empire is collapsing as Constantinople is taken by the Turks (1453). Nicholas of Cusa, who had been there in 1437, had just brought the frightful news back from Rome, and amidst the rumours of horrors, violence and blood everywhere, he wrote, one month before *On The Vision of God*, his *On the Peace of Faith*, an anti-Babelian vision of a heavenly theatre in which, one after another, a delegate from each nation gets up to bear witness to the movement which supports it. Greek, Italian, Arab, Indian, Chaldean, Jew, Scythian, Gaul, Persian, Syrian, Turk, Spaniard, German, Tartar, Armenian, and so forth, each one comes to attest in the language of his own tradition to the truth which is one: this harmony of 'free spirits' answers the furies of fanaticism.[16]

It is this *Vision of God* to which de Certeau refers, widely considered Nicholas's literary masterpiece,[17] that will draw our attention here. In my mind's eye, I can imagine Nicholas offering it as a model for the value of how CPE encourages group reflection; listening to new and different perspectives.

---

15. Sarton, *Six Wings*, 97.
16. De Certeau, "Gaze of Nicholas of Cusa," 3.
17. Hopkins, *Nicholas*, 44.

NICHOLAS OF CUSA'S VISION OF GOD

Nicholas corresponded frequently with a community of Christian monks at St Quirin's Monastery in Tegernsee, which fell within his bishopric of Brixen. The monks wrote in 1453 to ask Cardinal Cusa for his help in answering a question that had been troubling them: How may we know God? Behind the question lay a debate about mystical theology. Is it our heart or our mind that enables knowledge of God? Put another way, is it the affections or intellect where we are open, or opened to an understanding of God? It is hard to miss the fact that both options, heart or mind, and a third option if we choose to see it, heart and mind, are focused on the individual. So Nicholas decided that he would offer the monks a lesson on the importance of appreciating multiple perspectives. He answered their question with a small book, which he titled *On the Vision of God*. Nicholas also designed an exercise for the monks to undertake together before reading the book. The centerpiece of the exercise was an image of an all-seeing face.

"How can we know God?" the monks had asked. Nicholas instructed them to set the image of the all-seeing face against a wall in their monastery and form a semicircle around it. Nicholas asked the monks, first of all, to stand in that semicircle and look upon the image in silence, as if looking into the very face of God. In this first moment, he hoped that each monk would perceive "how diligently [the gaze] is concerned for each one of them, as if it were concerned for no one else; but only for him who experiences that he is seen. . . . To the brother who is situated in the east, it will seem as if the face is looking to the east; to the brother in the south, that the face is looking to the south."[18]

Next, Nicholas asked the monks to walk from one side of the image to the other, still in silence, and keeping their eyes fixed at all times on the face. In this second moment, he hoped that each monk would perceive that the gaze never leaves him, not even while he is moving. "Next, let the brother who was in the east situate himself in the west, and he will experience the gaze fixed on him in the west, just as it had previously been in the east."[19]

As affecting as those first two stages might have been, it is with the third stage of the exercise that Nicholas hoped the monks would perceive an even more striking discovery; a discovery they could not make by themselves. In their third and final act around the icon, Nicholas asked the

---

18. Preface to *De visione Dei*, para. 3–4.
19. Preface to *De visione Dei*, para. 3.

monks to break their silence and speak with one another about what they had experienced. In this moment, as they entered dialogue, Nicholas hoped the monks would learn that the all-seeing gaze had followed every one of them, even those who had been moving in opposite directions. "Through the disclosure of [his fellow brothers], each monk will come to know that the gaze does not desert anyone—not even those who are moving in contrary directions."[20]

LEARNING TO TRUST FRESH PERSPECTIVES

Nicholas's exercise is only that, a staged event in which *seeing* is an analogy for *knowing*. Yet there is something in this para-liturgy. Whereas the monks could see, while standing in silence, or silently moving from side to side, that the omnivoyant gaze was always resting upon them personally, the insight that the gaze was resting simultaneously upon them all was dependent on listening to one another and trusting what was heard from different perspectives. How may we know God? Yes, we may know something of God on our own. However, the third stage of this little play releases its simple yet profound insight. The gaze of God can feel so generous upon us that we might mistakenly assume we are its sole recipients, or that ours is the single point from which to gain a correct perspective. Yet, as we listen with trust to those who gain their perspective from other places, we begin to attain an even fuller vision of the One who sees us all. Only by listening to the perspective of those who stand in a different place do we begin to perceive that there are things invisible to us that are yet visible to them. Taking this observation one step further, our very awareness of the possibility of the presence of that which is invisible comes only if we are willing to trust those who see things differently.

The Tegernsee monks were invited to trust that the path to the knowledge of God is a mystery analogous to their experience around the image of God. There, each brother comes to the realization that he sees and is seen by the gaze regardless of where he stands. Further, on hearing his fellow monks declare that they too have been held by the gaze, regardless of where they stood, he also begins to perceive that there is a deeper wisdom available than he had initially been able to comprehend. The gaze in which they all feel held is one and the same gaze. It sees them all, regardless of their location. And so, although all see the face, and all feel themselves seen,

---

20. Preface to *De visione Dei*, para. 4.

the vision of God they each obtain is a contraction of the whole; a limited perspective. As the monks begin speaking with each other, and only in that moment, do they come to realize there is an excess; an excess that, by his sight alone, no single monk can comprehend. The valuable heuristic insight follows. Only dialogue allows each participant to understand that he sees merely a part of the whole; God is greater than any single perspective can encompass. Hearing from many perspectives will allow the knowledge of God to deepen.

CONCLUSION

We have been discussing CPE and Nicholas of Cusa's idea about how to obtain knowledge of God; in particular, the iconic exercise from his book *On the Vision of God*. The differences between the fifteenth-century cardinal and CPE's field-based pastoral practices are obvious and must not be understated. CPE is a program for people learning about their pastoral identity and the practice of ministry; a period of field-based learning, under an experienced supervisor, with a cohort of fellow students. Nicholas, on the other hand, was hoping to teach a group of Christian monks how to deepen their knowledge of God. He did that via an exercise which demonstrates the value of engaging with different points of view. Yet amid the clear differences, some commonality does come into view.

First, there is respect for each individual and their particular point of view and a recognition that individuals are set within a web of relationships. Second, there is acknowledgment that every participant—whether one of Nicholas's monks or a CPE student observing and participating in a pastoral situation—brings a particular perspective to her or his observations of the world. Every perspective has integrity. Yet each person's perspective is necessarily limited. Thus, everyone can be helped by hearing from different perspectives. Finally, among the most helpful aspects of Nicholas's exercise around the image of an all-seeing face is its demonstration of the epistemological significance of the other.[21] What do we mean by that? We

21. My use of the term "the other" is more pragmatic than the occasionally obsessive engagement with alterity. Rather, my use of the term is simply to acknowledge that, in the face of the other, we become relational and responsible, are made aware of our contracted place and of the risk of betraying our perspective, along with that of others, should we pretend to have a totality of vision or knowledge and, finally, it is also in the face of another that we become open to the possibilities vested in the idea of infinity. See "Facing the Other," in Barnes, *Theology and the Dialogue of Religions*, 65–96.

learn from that which is otherwise to our current perspective. We learn from difference. What we learn may serve to confirm or contradict our current perspective and yet, either way, we learn from hearing fresh perspectives. Knowledge is reformed and refined by our encounter with a living human document, with their web of relationships, and yet that knowledge is enhanced significantly by discussing those experiences with colleagues. To assume our perspective is the only reservoir of truth not only impedes our search for understanding, it jeopardizes that search altogether. For by placing our trust in a single point of view, we assume an absolute status for a posture which is finite and, therefore, inherently limited.

That the human search for understanding is enhanced by drawing differing perspectives into conversation is the central lesson of Nicholas's experiment and is, to my mind, the most significant gift to me of the CPE experience. Having established an awareness of the epistemological significance of the other, Nicholas also demonstrates the epistemological significance of dialogue; the value, if we truly wish to deepen knowledge, of listening to diverse points-of-view. In becoming aware of the different perspectives held by those who see (and are seen) by the all-seeing face, each participant becomes aware of the merit in establishing a habit of shared observation. That, too, was the legacy of the CPE experience to me: establishing the habit of sharing the challenges of pastoral ministry with a small and trusted group of colleagues. We all became more effective in ministry, and better able to carry the joys and challenges of our pastoral responsibilities, than we could ever have been alone.

BIBLIOGRAPHY

Anderson, Robert G. "The Integration of Clinical Pastoral Education with Seminary Learning: Fostering the Students Ministry Formation." *Journal of Pastoral Care* 50 (1996) 13–21.

Barnes, Michael. *Theology and the Dialogue of Religions.* Cambridge: Cambridge University Press, 2002.

Boisen, Anton T. *Out of the Depths.* New York: Harper, 1960.

De Certeau, Michel. "The Gaze of Nicholas of Cusa." *Diacritics* 17 (1987) 2–38.

Duclow, Donald. "Life and Work." In *Introducing Nicholas of Cusa: A Guide to a Renaissance Man*, edited by Christopher M. Bellitto, 25–56. New Jersey: Paulist, 2004.

Hopkins, Jasper. *Nicholas of Cusa's Dialectical Mysticism: Text, Translation and Interpretive Study.* 3rd ed. Minneapolis: Banning, 1996.

Meuthen, Erich. *Nicholas of Cusa: A Sketch for a Biography.* Translated by David Crowner and Gerald Christianson. Washington: Catholic University Press, 2010.

Miller-McLemore, Bonnie J. "The Living Human Web: Pastoral Theology at the Turn of the Century." In *Through the Eyes of Women: Insights for Pastoral Care*, edited by Jeanne Stevenson Moessner, 9–26. Minneapolis: Fortress, 1996.

———. "Revisiting the Living Web: Theological Education and the Role of Clinical Pastoral Education." *Journal of Pastoral Care and Counseling* 62 (2008) 3–17.

Monaco, Davide. *Nicholas of Cusa: Trinity, Freedom and Dialogue*. Munster: Aschendorff Verlag, 2016.

Sarton, George. *Six Wings: Men of Science in the Renaissance*. Madison: University of Wisconsin Press, 1959.

Theruvathu, Prasad J. N. *Ineffabilis in the Thought of Nicholas of Cusa*. Munster: Aschendorff Verlag, 2010.

3

Co-creation

A Model for Clinical Pastoral Education and Supervision

Jennifer Washington

ADULT LEARNING THEORY ENCOURAGES educators to engage with students in a mutual, collaborative process, recognizing the knowledge, skills, and experience of the adult learner. In this process the educator/teacher considers and is curious about how the students' prior experience offers insights into their new learning experience. Within the context of clinical pastoral education, pastoral supervision is offered by a more experienced practitioner to a beginner. This paper explores frameworks that have evolved over twenty years informing an experienced practitioner in providing pastoral supervision to support beginning supervisors and pastoral practitioners to draw from, integrate, and build upon their prior learning experience. In this mutual, collaborative model knowledge and skills are co-created.

As an educator I believe that new insights can develop when we take time to reflect upon an experience; to note our observations, wonder about, explore our thoughts and feelings, and examine more closely the assumptions we bring to the experience. It is a challenging task to notice let alone examine our taken for granted assumptions. Nearness to our own experience can have us caught in our own limited ways of thinking and processing. Supervision provides an opportunity to expand the lens, to view the event from another, different perspective. In supervision we engage with another who was not present in the originating experience. The task of the supervisor is to act as a container, holding open the space for the event to be heard, held, and thought about, to offer another perspective, to work with the supervisee to create a deeper understanding of what was occurring for the patient, the spiritual carer and the presenting concern.

As we seek to make sense of our world, theories attempt to provide us with frameworks or lens through which we can describe and or predict something. They also enable us to understand or reason as to why something happened. The theory that I will present in this paper is the theory of co-creation: a model for clinical pastoral education and supervision.

WHAT DO I MEAN BY CO-CREATION?

At the heart of co-creation is a belief that God is intimately involved in the world, continually calling it forth into being. In the Scriptures we are reminded of God's faithfulness and love for all creation. In and through Jesus we come to understand that God's desire for creation is that we may "have life and have it abundantly."[1] This in an invitation to embrace life, to be alive to life, alive in our relationships with one another and to our world. Winnicott speaks of aliveness as feeling real, living creatively and spontaneously, in ways that reflect one's true self, with capacity for trust and faith in relationships that offer meaning and ongoing experiences of feeling alive and real.[2]

EMBRACING LIFE

To explore what it means to embrace life I will draw from Miroslov Volf's work. He believes that embrace involves four deliberate movements: opening one's arms, waiting, closing arms, and opening arms again. Volf states that the movement to open our arms is a sign of discontent with our own self-enclosed identity. It is a desire for the other. Open arms are a sign that I have created space in myself for the other to come in and that I have made a movement out of myself so as to enter the space created by the other. As

---

1. John 10:10.
2. Kuchan, "Prayer," 266, citing Winnicott, *Home Is Where We Start From*.

a supervisor educator how do I create space in myself for my students? In doing this how does this modeling invite my students to also open their arms, make space for new thoughts, ideas to enter into them? What happens when I'm met with resistance?

Volf states that the second movement is waiting. He writes, "If embrace takes place, it will always be because the other has desired the self just as the self has desired the other."[3] Waiting allows for reciprocity. This is a place of vulnerability, we wait not knowing how the other will respond, will they be open to us, to what we may offer them?

The third movement is one in which the arms are closed, each is both holding and being held by the other, both active and passive, a host is a guest and a guest is a host. Though one self may receive or give more than the other, each must enter the space of the other, feel the presence of the other in the self, and make its own presence felt. In an embrace the identity of the self is both preserved and transformed, and the alterity of the other is both affirmed as alterity (otherness) and partly received into the ever-changing identity of the self. The self understands that what there is to understand about the other can "only be addressed as a question."

In the final movement that of opening the arms again, the other must be let go so that her alterity—her genuine dynamic identity—may be preserved; and the self must take itself back into itself so that its own identity, enriched by the traces that the presence of the other has left, may be preserved.

CREATIVITY

In this next section I will explore what it means to be creative, to co-create. I have come that you may have life and have it abundantly, comes as an invitation, a calling in which we are invited to respond.

Creativity follows art more closely than science. It is unpredictable, chaotic, and serendipitous, moments of inspiration are absolutely essential.[4]

---

3. Volf, *Exclusion and Embrace*, 142–43.
4. Rill and Hämäläinen, *Art of Co-creation*.

CO-CREATION IS COLLABORATIVE

Michael Schrage, author of *Shared Minds*, states that co-creation is possible when real collaboration takes place. He describes collaboration as

> the process of shared creation: where two or more individuals with complementary skills interact to create a shared understanding that none had previously possessed or could have come to on their own. Collaboration creates a shared meaning about a process, a product, or an event[5]

Co-creation does not require consensus, which is very difficult to achieve with diverse groups. Instead, it requires empowerment.[6]

In and through the supervisory relationship we have an opportunity to creatively engage with supervisees or students, to change and grow as individuals and in our practice as we explore together pastoral situations. This opportunity for creativity extends beyond the supervisory relationship to the pastoral relationship where both student pastor and patient may experience the opportunity, invitation to be changed through their engagement in deep listening and creative dialogue.

Collaboration is distinct from communication, coordination, and cooperation. Collaboration is not about exchanging information it is about using information to create something new. Unlike coordination, collaboration seeks divergent insight and spontaneity, not structural harmony. And unlike cooperation, collaboration thrives on differences and requires the sparks of dissent.[7]

Creativity requires newness. It requires us entering into the unknown and exploring the potential that lies therein. I will explore the potential of this co-creative space that exists between learning from one's experience and learning from others: whether that is in the person of the supervisor, our engagement with the wider professional knowledge or in a discussion of the literature with our supervisor as we seek to find creative ways, ways that will be life enhancing, in response to the issues and concerns of the people we meet through ministry.

---

5. Rill and Hämäläinen, *Art of Co-creation*, 23.
6. Rill and Hämäläinen, *Art of Co-creation*, 24.
7. Rill and Hämäläinen, *Art of Co-creation*, 24.

Part I: History, Framework, and Theology

APPROACHES TO LEARNING: INDUCTIVE AND DEDUCTIVE

At teachers' college I was introduced to a variety of educational theorists and theories. John Dewey's theories about experiential learning resonated. I found things easier to learn if I could see how it could be applied in practice. As a teacher-in-training I was encouraged to develop lessons that not only actively engaged students in their learning, but also provided them with the opportunity to discover something new for themselves, to experience the joy of creativity and creative engagement. In a lesson on movement, I sourced from the local butcher bones showing ball-and-socket as well as hinge joints. While being a great hit with the forty-plus year-six boys who had a hands-on experience manipulating the joints, seeing how they worked, they were also able to understand how the different joints in their bodies functioned in order to create movement.

In my experience, teachers' college was theory driven, a top-down approach where I was encouraged to apply theory to practice. Here I learned a variety of theories and methodologies. Teaching reading is a good example. Theories about teaching reading enabled teachers' choice and provided alternatives if the theory being used was failing with a student or a group of students. This experience points to a bigger theory that invited us to see that not all students would learn in the same way or at the same pace. Learning strategies would need to be individualized, developed, and creatively respond to the needs and abilities of the students. This was an ideal that presented an unrealistic challenge given that most classrooms had thirty or more students.

My next formal learning experience came when I commenced clinical pastoral education. This model placed an even greater emphasis on experience. Within the first week I was introduced to several wards in the hospital as the chaplain for the "non-Catholic" patients. In this sink-or-swim approach, experience became the teacher. In not knowing the patients' medical condition I learned to listen to the patients' experience of illness, and of being in hospital. They were the experts in themselves and in their understanding of their condition. As wards specialized in diagnosing and treating particular illnesses, I noticed reoccurring patterns not only in patients' experience but also in the way the ward functioned. In reflecting on patient's experience through the supervisory relationship I was beginning to learn to listen deeply and respond to the unique needs of the other while also building theories. These theories were about what it meant to be human: about suffering, pain, loss, helplessness, vulnerability, interdependence, hope, faith, courage, and what it meant to be pastoral. This model of learning is a more inductive, bottom up, approach. A theory that evolves from experience.

As each new experience involved engaging with another in pastoral ministry there was always within it, the potential for something unexpected or new to occur. For a novice this is both exciting and challenging. The bottom-up approach provides an opportunity to reflect upon, notice, to be curious about, and to wonder. In this approach experience is taken seriously. In dialoguing with another we may begin the process of recognizing and examining the knowledge and underlying assumptions that we bring to an experience. This knowing is drawn from our engagement in the world and the wisdom of those who have gone before us, those who have reflected and built theories about what it means to be pastoral. At this point we are aware of and engaged at the intersection of the bottom-up and top-down approaches to learning. Each feeds the other. Potentially, theories are tested, expanded, challenged, reshaped, created.

As a CPE supervisor and an educator of CPE supervisors I believe that the challenge is how to keep both a top-down and bottom-up approach working in critical dialogue. One that provides students with language to speak of their experience and what they often do intuitively, while at the same time paying attention to the uniqueness of the person or persons and this ministry or supervisory event. Theories enable us to explore our experience, but they are not the experience. It is important to note the things that are not explained or lie outside of the theory so that we respond to the uniqueness of the person. We all hold various theories, some of these theories are held consciously while others are unconscious. In supervision we have the opportunity to examine our theories, to uncover those that are unconscious, to explore our assumptions, as these assumptions guide and at times can limit our practice.

When I have felt lost and not sure how to respond or work with a student, theories have provided ideas, they have supported me with some insights and helped guide me in how to work or respond to a situation.

If we only have a few theories then, it is likely that we will interpret our experience through this limited range. The danger here is that we may miss the nuances and complexity of the ministry or supervisory event. In reflecting upon the "History of the Clinical Pastoral Education Movement" the movement has been influenced by its engagement with theory, or theories:

theories developed by theologians, including practical theologians, psychology and counseling, educational theorists, sociology, and in healthcare settings, medicine.

THEORIES THAT HAVE INFORMED MY PRACTICE?

As a beginning supervisor I leapt into the deep, planning and conducting an eleven-week full-time CPE program with five participants. In preparation, I read David Steer's book on pastoral supervision and gained a few ideas that helped me navigate this exciting and challenging opportunity. With the assistance and support of a wise and experienced supervisor,[8] I was invited to a deeper reflection upon the student's observations of the patient and the patients' story presented in their verbatims,[9] and from there to identify the students' learning needs.[10] In reflecting together, I experienced my supervisor come alongside me and help me develop greater empathy for the patient, as well as an ability to identify student's learning edges and a model for supervision; one where I could similarly come alongside my students and assist them to develop greater empathic understanding of the patients to whom they ministered.

PRIMACY OF THE RELATIONSHIP

As a child I learned to play the piano. Learning to play any new piece of music required hours of practice, stumbling over keys, stretching my fingers to find new keys, repeating sections until I could play that part with some level of proficiency and then more hours to learn to play the piece as

---

8. During my first years of supervisory education, Rev. Keith Little invited me to develop an understanding of Melanie Klein's object-relations theory. This theory discusses the effect of the internalized relations with primary caretakers during infancy (i.e., objects), and their unconscious influence on the nature of future relationships. The infant internalizes two sets of object relations—both positive and negative—which include representations of the self, the object, and the emotion that links between the two. (See https://www.learning-theories.com/object-relations-theory-melanie-klein.html.)

9. Mode 1 in Hawkins and Shohet's seven-eyed process model of supervision focuses on the patient, what the pastor noticed or observed about the patient and the patient's story, their current situation, diagnosis, etc.

10. Modes 2 and 3, Hawkins and Shohet. In mode 2, the focus is upon the interventions which can also uncover unknown or hidden aspects of the therapeutic relationship. Mode 3 focuses on the patient-pastor relationship.

a whole and then with feeling. Often my music teacher would introduce a new piece of music by playing it, letting me know how it sounded. One day when I was struggling to get the rhythm of the music, my teacher took me by the hand, and we moved around the room to the beat—to feel it bodily. This is a powerful model for supervision. Through the process of modeling, breaking things down into manageable steps, patience, encouragement, and creativity I was enabled to succeed, to experience the joy of playing a piece of music.

At the heart of my model of supervision and pastoral ministry as co-creation is the "call" to develop an empathic understanding of the person that we are working with and the situation in which they find themselves. I deliberately use the word *called* as I believe that for our own flourishing and for the flourishing of the other, we need to move beyond self-preoccupation. We are called to move out of our own small confines, to use our imagination, our thoughts and sensitivity to wonder about what it's like to stand in the other person's shoes. In doing this we develop empathy for the person. We can then explore our thoughts about the person's emotional and spiritual needs, identifying resources that they have before thinking creatively about various ways in which the pastor could respond. Similarly, the supervisor is called to build an empathic understanding of their student in order to understand the impact that the ministry event had on the student, the resources that they brought to the event and their learning issues, edges in terms of knowledge, skills or attitudes.

Each person in the process brings to supervision the richness and messiness of their previous experience, knowledge, skills, beliefs, and assumptions. The role of the supervisor is to hold open the space for deeper reflection while also entering it. Having used the reflective process it is a reasonable expectation that the supervisor brings to this encounter a deeper level of intra-personal awareness as well as interpersonal skills and awareness. The supervisor's role is to use their knowledge and skills for the benefit of the other. If we can hold open the space, suspend judgment then it is possible that new thoughts, ideas, awareness, insights can occur for both supervisee and supervisor. This is the co-creative space, where in dialogue we refuse to settle for only one interpretation but continue to hold open, explore our thoughts, images, feelings, assumptions, ideas to potentially create a new understanding. Both supervisor and supervisee are changed through their encounter.

In supervision we enter into a covenant with the supervisee. Volf states that "covenant is not simply a relationship of mutual utility, but of moral commitment. Because covenant is lasting, the parties themselves cannot be conceived of as individuals whose identities are external to one another and who are related to one another only by virtue of moral will and moral practice. Rather, the very identity of each is formed through relation to others; the alterity of the other enters into the very identity of each."[11] Volf invites us to see that we are being formed and reformed through our commitment to genuine dialogue. He states that we are constantly called to renew the covenant. This means to attend to the shifts in the identity of the other, to make space for the changing other in ourselves, and to be willing to re-negotiate our own identity in interaction with the fluid identity of the other. In and through the supervisory relationship we are engaged in a change process, we are challenged and invited to see anew, to hear different perspectives, to examine our assumptions, to let go of our desire to over control things and dare to take a risk in responding in a new and different way.

Volf states that "sustaining and renewing covenants between persons and groups requires the work of mutual 'making space for the other in the self' and of re-arranging the self in light of other's presence."[12] How do I make space for the supervisee in myself, how am I re-arranging my-self in the light or their presence?

Supervision as co-creation recognizes the importance of establishing a welcoming, hospitable environment for learning to occur. The affective experience of learning is probably the most powerful determinant of learning. Boud and Miller remind us that "emotions can also act as substantial barriers" to learning.[13] Anger and fear limit what the student is able to hear. These emotions need to be recognized and attended to before the student can engage in a creative dialogue, wonder, explore, and learn.

WHAT IS LEARNING?

Jarvis defines learning as "the process in which the 'whole person' engages in an experience that is processed cognitively, emotively or practically (or

---

11. Volf, *Exclusion and Embrace*, 154.
12. Volf, *Exclusion and Embrace*, 153.
13. Boud, "Animating Learning," 17.

through any combination) and integrated into the person's individual biography resulting in a change (or more experienced) person."[14]

Learning involves every aspect of our personhood. Learning a new skill, such as riding a bike, involves more than the mechanics of balance, peddling, and steering; thinking and judgment are required as we navigate the road. Our emotions are involved, we experience fear when the bike wobbles, as we manage our fear, we gain better balance and a sense of control. Learning a new skill is deeply satisfying, it affects our sense of self, our identity, thus it is also spiritual.

The Latin word for educate is *educere*, meaning to lead out or draw out. In approaching any new experience, adults bring to it knowledge, skills, attitudes, beliefs, and assumptions from our past. These all shape the lens through which we view and understand our present experience.

Each person has within themselves thoughts, impressions, feelings that are related to their experience, some knowing that can be drawn upon, examined, explored. It is likely that they have already made some assumptions about their experience as they process it and seek to make sense, meaning. If the new experience has not been disruptive, the process occurs without much conscious attention. Disruptive events,[15] such as serious illness, may require much more and can lead to a shattering of one's worldview, it may also in time lead to a new understanding, a perspective change, the construction of a new worldview that allows space for the integration of this disruptive experience. As meaning making, seeking beings we desire to bring a sense of coherence to our story. In engaging in ministry our students encounter events that they find disruptive, our role as a supervisor is to support them through their process; to seek to understand what is occurring for them, to be a dialogue partner, to offer them our thoughts, perspective, to journey with them as they travel in unknown territory. Our theories help us in this endeavour of turning a disruptive event into a "teachable moment."[16]

14. Merriam and Bierema, *Adult Learning*, 112.

15. Dewey named these events a precarious event. By that he meant an event that somehow makes an ongoing experience problematic, thus, any obstacle, disruption, danger, or surprise of any kind is precarious. Mezirow speaks of a disruptive event and believes these can lead to transformation. He provides a map involving a ten-step process. Merriam notes that from a transformative learning perspective, adult educators are change agents. They note that few educators are trained to handle the discomfort, angst, and conflict that often accompany making changes (Merriam and Bierema, *Adult Learning*, 101).

16. Havighurst, *Developmental Tasks and Education*, cited in Merriam and Bierema, *Adult Learning*, 50.

Part I: History, Framework, and Theology

SOME HELPFUL THEORIES

As supervision and education are both complex, it is helpful to have the assistance of a range of theories. In this section I would like to list a few that I have found helpful and that I believe fit with the model of supervision as co-creation.

Inskipp and Proctor identify three supervisory functions, they are; formative (educative), normative (administrative) and restorative (supportive).[17] These functions help us to hold in awareness the breadth of the supervisor's role. The supervisor's role is to discern which function or combination will provide the optimal learning, holding experience for the supervisee.

Peter L. VanKatwyk's *Helping Style Inventory* provides a framework from which we can reflect upon and identify our supervisory interventions. It invites us to explore our use of power and the focus of our attention. We can use the inventory to discern other ways of working, responding.

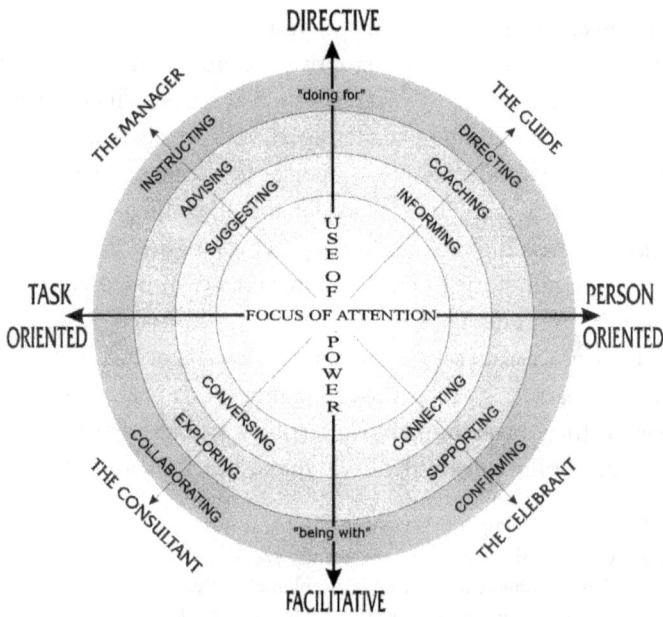

The Helping Style Inventory. Reprinted by permission from Vankatwyk (2010, fig. 3).

---

17. Inskipp and Proctor, *Art, Craft & Tasks*; in brackets I have included the names of these functions as identified by Kadushin, *Supervision in Social Work*.

Jarvis provides another map in which he identifies four approaches to teaching:

- Didactic; teachers expound the knowledge to be learned by students, this is a top-down approach.
- Socratic; teachers lead students toward a conclusion to their enquiry by shrewd questioning.
- Facilitative; teachers create conditions under which learning can occur, but they do not seek to control its outcome.
- Experiential; teachers seek to provide learners with experiences which involve the whole person, an example would be role play.

In these teaching approaches Jarvis provides language that can help to identify supervisory interventions. No approach is necessarily better than another. The choice of approach is important to be made in response to the supervisee's learning stage and need. Inherent in each is the exercise of the supervisor's authority and power. How are we using our power and authority as a supervisor to form and create a context for supervision that engenders co-creation?

CONCLUSION

John Norcross reminds us that "the (supervisor) needs to develop expertise in forming a strong alliance, empathy, adapting methods to the (supervisee's) preferences and culture, providing skilled interventions, eliciting (supervisee) feedback and making appropriate adjustments in response to such feedback."[18]

Supervision as co-creation places an emphasis on learning from experience, engaging in a critical dialogue, hunting down and checking assumptions, staying open to see, consider things from different perspectives and using our insights to inform our action. In a co-creative model the supervisee and supervisor risk being changed through the engagement. They have the opportunity to respond to the call *I have come that you may have life and have it abundantly.*

---

18. Norcross, *Psychotherapy Relationships at Work*, cited in Hewson and Carroll, *Reflective Practice*, 226. I have substituted the words *supervisor* and *supervisee* for *practitioner* and *client* as appears in the original quote.

BIBLIOGRAPHY

Boud, David, and Nod Miller. "Animating Learning from Experience." In *Working with Experience: Animating Learning*, edited by David Boud and Nod Miller, 3–13. London: Routledge, 1996.

Havighurst, Robert J. *Developmental Tasks and Education*. 3rd ed. New York: McKay, 1972.

Hewson, Daphne, and Michael Carroll. *Reflective Practice in Supervision*. Hazelbrook, Australia: Moshpit, 2016.

Inskipp, Francesca, and Brigid Proctor. *The Art, Craft & Tasks of Counselling Supervision*. Vol. 1, *Making the Most of Supervision*. Twickenham, UK: Cascade, 1993.

Jarvis, Peter. "Adults Learning—Some Theorists' Perspectives." In *Adult Education and Lifelong Learning: Theory and Practice*. 3rd ed. London: RoutledgeFalmer, 2004.

Kadushin, Alfred. *Supervision in Social Work*. New York: Columbia University Press, 1976.

Kuchan, Karen. "Prayer as Therapeutic Process toward Aliveness within a Spiritual Direction Relationship." *Journal of Religion and Health* 47 (2008) 263–75.

Leach, Jane, and Michael Paterson. *Pastoral Supervision: A Handbook*. London: SCM, 2010.

Merriam, Sharan B., and Laura L. Bierema. *Adult Learning: Linking Theory and Practice*. San Francisco: Jossey-Bass, 2014.

Norcross, John, ed. *Psychotherapy Relationships at Work*. New York: Oxford University Press, 2011.

Rill, Bryan R., and Matti M. Hämäläinen. *The Art of Co-creation: A Guidebook for Practitioners*. Singapore: Palgrave Macmillan, 2018.

VanKatwyk, Peter L. "Supervision as Critical Clinical Reflection." *Canadian Association for Spiritual Care*. Last modified 2010. http://www.spiritualcare.ca/flow/uploads/docs/Supervision_Critical_Reflection.pdf.

Volf, Miroslav. *Exclusion and Embrace: A Theological Exploration of Identity, Otherness, and Reconciliation*. Nashville: Abingdon, 1996.

Winnicott, Donald. *Home Is Where We Start From: Essays by a Psychoanalyst*. New York: Norton, 1990.

4

Prospecting for Grace in the Secular World of CPE

R. Dean Drayton

CLINICAL PASTORAL EDUCATION (CPE) provides resources for pastoral practitioners to relate to people in crisis times of life and help both the visitor and the visited be aware of the meaning and purpose that they give to their life. Courses and training focus on helping the pastoral visitor establish a respectful presence and relationship with a person being visited. Such a presence may open the way for life's joys and issues to be explored, personal dynamics considered and the spiritual aspects of life to be addressed.

The aim of clinical pastoral education is to clear the way for the pastoral visitor to be the most effective presence that they can be for the person visited. In the course work and the visits, the practitioner is brought to face their own particular approach and attitude toward others. Through visits, the preparation of verbatims, and structured and informal reflection with others on what happened in the visits they have made, they find out some of the distinctiveness of their own approach and attitude toward others. In this learning context the visitor is helped to become aware of the ways they can offer greater attention and share insights with the one visited.

It can be confronting for the pastoral person to learn in the course how much their approach is predisposed to their own issues—distracted by their own perspectives, not hearing what the other is actually saying, in a way that limits their awareness of the other's life situation. This relearning of interaction with others is not easy. It pays off, however in the way the discoveries made help the CPE visitor to be present with the person visited. It is this release of a new quality of relationship that provides the experiential space for pastoral sharing, a place for questions of purpose to arise, and an arena for sharing and exploring the spiritual dimension in life.

The formal and informal training involved in CPE provides accreditation for those whose task it is to work in the public arena. The practitioners are made very much aware that they are working in a secular world. There are clear boundaries as to what can be asked of a person or shared with a person visited in any public institution. The rights and the freedom of the person visited must be not only respected, but honoured. These values are even more important in situations where a person is not well, or incapacitated in some form. A visit is not an opportunity for preaching at a person or asking private and intrusive questions of a person's life or attitudes. The CPE visitor is taught to be aware of the power differential between visitor and visited that is implicit in all relationships in such settings in which a person with skills and accredited authority of some kind is meeting with a person whose freedom is curtailed by their illness or the situation in which they find themselves.

VISITING IN A SECULAR SETTING

This description of the setting of pastoral visiting raises a serious question. How is it possible for the CPE visitor to encourage spiritual practices and approaches when it is not possible to assume such practices and approaches are accepted or given credence by the person visited? The CPE visitor has to carefully negotiate this awkward boundary between the spiritual and the secular, between the religious and the ordinary. It is not that these matters cannot be discussed or shared, but in this secular setting it is vital that such interaction be with the invitation and permission of the person visited. Over centuries and more recently decades those involved in pastoral visitation have had to continually adapt to the way the religious realm interacts with the changes in the wider society. Holifield in his *History of Pastoral Care in America* documents the long-term move from salvation to self-realization under the impact of the democratic era's stress on self-actualization and fulfillment moving away from the former emphasis on sin and forgiveness.[1] It was in 1966 that Philip Rieff prophetically described what has become ever more evident, the increasing emphasis of the therapeutic role in pastoral care.[2] And importantly, since so much depends on the quality of the listening in establishing a pastoral relationship how is that related to the biblical message? Pattison is one who has pointed out the strange silence of the Bible with regard to this core matter.[3]

In the light of such a complex history and changing perspectives the CPE visitor needs to be aware of their own approach and convictions that they bring to conversations about matters of spirituality and spiritual practice. In nearly every case, the visitor knows little of the long history of pastoral care in the church, and takes for granted the views of this denominational religious age that emerged as a result of the Enlightenment.

Within this perspective there are a range of options that are derived from this form of the church. Are they religiously conservative or liberally open in their approach to belief and sacred books? Do they stress the importance of individual motivation and purpose in life, or are they more concerned with the rights of the individual? Is their life story grounded in the predominant culture of the society or among those who are on the edge of social interaction? In a multicultural and multi-faith environment, how do they relate to people of other faiths with different religious understanding and experience? Each of these options impact on the way the religious dimension is approached, and the way questions are framed about religion and God. In our time, each of the options disclose elements of this move toward a therapeutic form of visitation. Whether articulated or not, there are consequences for the particular way the visitor relates to those who are visited.

But further, the pastoral context is constrained by the fact that conversations in this religious zone, one on one, are considered to be private and confidential. Once more this is a consequence of a generally accepted belief that these are fundamentally private matters.

Given this background and the restrictions that flow from the nature of CPE and these boundary conditions in a secular setting, what then are

---

1. Holifield, *History of Pastoral Care*.
2. Reiff, *Triumph of the Therapeutic*.
3. Pattison, *Critique of Pastoral Care*. See ch. 6, "The Bible and Christian Care," and an extended discussion of this matter.

the ways that a person who is a CPE trained visitor can be present to helpfully explore the dimension of religious spiritual practice in the chaplaincy setting?

The following discussion is for Christians who are involved as CPE visitors but because of the nature of the setting may well be relevant for other Abrahamic faiths especially.

TWO POLES OF A RELIGIOUS CONTINUUM

Generally for Christian CPE visitors there are two predominant ways that spiritual matters and God are usually brought into the discussion with the person visited when religious issues are discussed in the secular setting. As it turns out both of these perspectives are in themselves heavily influenced by the view and practice of religion in a secular world.

Both approaches presume the development of the relationship shared between the visited and CPE visitor in the sharing of life stories, vital experiences, crises, insights, hopes, and yearnings. The depth of the relationship that develops in this meeting depends upon so many factors in the life of the person visited; their health, the sort of day it is, their facility with words and feelings, and so many other unique and individual elements. As the two share it is possible for a growing appreciation for each other and a lessening in the reticence to share. This can happen with many words, or without words, as silences are shared together.

In the first approach the pastoral agent articulates a message or framework that they bring to the relationship. The key step depends on the ability of the pastoral visitor to listen and identify key experiences of the visited that have the potential to be explored in terms of religious themes, such as God, forgiveness, wonder, faith, promise, etc. This enables the pastoral agent to bring a sensitive and specific presentation of a spiritual message for the person that hopefully resonates with their life and context. The art is to be able to translate the message meaningfully for the person within the field of matters that have emerged in what has been shared. Thus the religious discussion is both derived and enriched by the word or message that is brought to the shared relationship by the pastoral worker.

The second approach puts the emphasis on the person visited being able to recognize critical moments, events or experiences that have been either vital to them, or rejected by them, as the basis for an understanding of religious matters. The focus is on exploring the religious dimension of the person. This they may articulate from their own experience, or may discover further from the conversation that ensues. The visitor's role is seen to be that of acknowledging the integrity of what has been shared, and providing further reflection from their own experience. There is no attempt to bring a particular message to them, rather the hope is to elicit from the person their own religious awareness in the situation they are facing.

Let us call the first the message approach, with a significant element of the message brought from outside the relationship, at its best, sensitively done, for the sake of the person within the relationship. In the second it is assumed that the task of discussion is to elicit from the person the understanding and experience of God that they already have, to whatever degree that is possible.

Both approaches, require careful listening and vulnerable sharing that is made possible by the space the clinical pastoral person makes possible. And yes, these are two poles of a continuum. It is vital for those doing CPE to know which mode is primary in their own approach to discussions about religious meaning and practice.

A CRITICAL ISSUE

It is important at this juncture to once again return to the assumptions that are implicit in this one on one relationship. The conversations focused on the person visited are private, confidential, and depend upon the person visited giving permission for such times. It is the only way to ensure that this sort of religious conversation can be held in secular settings. There is, however, a danger arising from the nature of this meeting space. The encounter is a highly individualized encounter, inevitably framed in personal and relational terms and must be so. Thus exploration and the articulation of the religious dimension is framed in these terms that allow the visited individual to either receive a message from the visitor or a chance to explore their own particular religious experience and understanding.

"What is wrong with this?" I can hear someone say. It seems patently obvious that this is the case and this is the aim of clinical pastoral counseling. This encounter, however, takes for granted a whole range of considerations that shape this one-to-one encounter within a very particular Enlightenment worldview in which the individual is the fundamental reference point. The process is focused on the individual, limiting spiritual language to the understanding and the experience of the visitor or the visited.

The result is that almost all the spiritual language available for realization in the relationship is centered in the self, whether heard from another or discovered within. The within/without categories are both the hallmark and the consequence of this secular age. The Enlightenment gives rise to life centered in the self, surrounded by a series of concentric circles, that spread out from this center into the society. It is the need to protect this sort of vulnerable self that gave rise to the boundaries that are required to protect such a conversation in a public place within this secular environment. An individual pastoral visitor is focused on the "within" of the individual from the perspective of one who is "without" in orbit about them.

The visitor and the visited also share common cultural understandings as to what is religion and religious discussion. In the West, religion is about the ten commandments, morality, and as a result, what it means to be good in some accepted way. It is not surprising that much religious discussion in this setting revolves around the assessment of a person's own personal history of relationships with parents, family, and immediate community. A person's own internal evaluation of their life almost inevitably involves an assessment of what they have done in terms of right and wrong. This is the nature of religious discussion for most in the community. It is not unusual for God to come into the conversation in terms of gratitude for life, an awareness of what needs to be put right, and often a sense of the absence of God, and various combinations of these.

Why is it a problem that these factors are built into a visit? It is a problem because the context for the visit pushes the relationship in a therapeutic direction. The role of the pastoral visit is to help the person being visited in ways that depend upon their particular circumstances. The visited person is the focus of attention in this process. It is a helping role, finding ways to meet with a person, affirming them in the meeting and where possible wanting the person to become more aware of their understanding and experience of the religious realm in their life. In hospitals, rehabilitation centers, sanatoriums, and other social institutions, this clinical pastoral role is attuned to the dominant direction of all that is being done there to help the person move along some scale toward greater health and healing. Within this quite structured setting, it is not surprising that CPE usually assumes a therapeutic model of operation.

Indeed when the individual self is at the center of the approach it is hard to envisage any other way of comprehending what is happening. After the visit, the visitor usually asks themselves whether their presence helped this person or not. Did the person make some steps in finding, unlocking or articulating a freedom in being more aware of their religious situation?

But what if the religious dimension is not primarily about therapy, whether in this particular boundary setting, or any other setting? The claim here is that seeing religious discussion as therapy is a reflection of the psychologizing tendencies endemic in the wider society that reflect the language of the self as the primary center of reference. This view is in fact a reduction of the fundamental reality of the religious dimension. It will be important then for clinical pastoral education to help develop ways to operate in the religious dimension in other than a therapeutic perspective.

It is not easy to disengage from a well-accepted way of operating. A radically new framework is confronting. It is not only clinical pastoral education that has been caught up in this therapeutic perspective. As a result of the Enlightenment, and the privatizing of religion, the church too has embraced a therapeutic approach in the way the gospel is shared and worship enacted.

The religious dimension is presented primarily in terms of separation from God and the way to overcome that separation. In the wider social community the religious dimension has come to be about God, sin, and forgiveness. It is quite common for people to say they are not religious, have questions about God, and see the church as irrelevant to their life.

People in hospital or other institutions find themselves in a liminal situation in their life with a new normal and routine with time to think and ponder. It is not surprising that the issue of forgiveness is often a point of contact and concern. It becomes clear that an unwillingness to let go the hurts and offence in key events with a key person or persons in the past, prevents a person from moving on in the religious dimension. It becomes clear there is often a need to *clean the slate* and move toward seeking forgiveness or reconciliation with key people. It can be a great step forward for the person, identifying and reassessing vital controlling and shaping relationships and the way to bring healing. For the CPE visitor this reassessment of past relationships by the person visited moves into an area that is on the boundaries of what is permissible in the secular milieu. With the permission of the person visited, this need or desire for forgiveness can then be framed in a particular spiritual way for them. Through the visitor's help, the person is then able to bring the issue before God. In this way God becomes an active agent in the therapy for the person visited.

Part I: History, Framework, and Theology

This *individual and God* relationship starts with the individual. It is taken for granted, both in the church and visitation in the Enlightenment and post Enlightenment eras, that this *me and God* relationship is the normal way it is. What, though, if this approach is in fact a distortion of the New Testament presentation of the relation between God and humanity?

Let us explore further this "normal" understanding of the relationship in the Christian community.

> A reading of the historical tradition of pastoral care makes it quite clear that, despite its varying forms, a constant underlying common denominator has been the struggle against sin and sorrow in whatever way it has arisen in personal or corporate life.[4]

In the *me and God* religious relationship it is accepted that a person needs to acknowledge their sins, repent of them, and bring them to God so that they can be forgiven by God and the relationship restored between God and the individual. The commonly accepted understanding of forgiveness is that when we have realized we have done something wrong, we should first repent of this, and then as it is often said, bring the sin to the cross of Jesus for forgiveness and leave it there. I remember one devotional teacher being asked how many times a day did she have to come to the cross—four or five times? No, came the answer that shocked the inquirer, a thousand times a day. It is presumed that the individual needs to take the initiative to recognize, repent, and approach the cross of Christ, God's place of forgiveness.

Here, God gives the solution to our issue. It is a move toward God who then forgives this particular matter. It is a form of spiritual therapy that the person undertakes.

This same approach is also deeply ingrained in the ritual form of the prayer of confession commonly heard in public worship. The liturgist spells out our sins communally, inviting the worshipper to acknowledge and identify how they are caught up in these practices and attitudes. Then at the end of the prayer forgiveness is given in a general way with the declaration that our sins are forgiven in the name of Christ. Both devotionally and communally these are both actually therapeutic models, outlining the way we participate to be forgiven.

---

4. Pattison, *Critique of Pastoral Care*, 13.

It is not surprising that in this time, when the individual is the fundamental reference point for life, that spiritual matters have been reframed in terms of the perspective of the individual.

THE FLOW IS FROM GOD TO US

What happens though if we look carefully at scripture and ask how forgiveness operates in the relation between God and the individual. It is radically different from what is the common understanding, and quite clearly it is not a therapeutic process.

The New Testament reverses the normal direction of the individual coming to God, and shows that it is the action of God reconciling a creation that includes the individual. It is the reverse of the traditional understanding. God initiates the action, not the individual!

Let us consider the important issue of forgiveness. The words forgive and forgiveness occur in the gospels and the letters of the New Testament about fifty times. A careful look at the relevant verses discloses a remarkable fact. The forgiveness passages are about the way God restores the relationship for people so that individuals can restore relationships with one another. One does not approach God and say, I am now sorry for what I have done, and ask forgiveness to receive forgiveness. Instead, one receives forgiveness to the degree the individual forgives those who have offended against them.

This God to us flow includes the individual. It can be summarized by the shorthand version of the dynamics as spelled out in Col 1:13.

> He [Jesus] has rescued us from the power of darkness and transferred us into the kingdom of his beloved Son, in whom we have redemption, the forgiveness of sins.

The forgiveness of sins has already happened in the death and resurrection and ascension of Jesus of Nazareth. The extraordinary unbelievable act is God's act, that has covered over our sins, before we ever asked or knew. God is at work in the situation wiping the slate clean, and in doing so helping us find that we stand in the grace of God. This is the good news. How then do we respond to this gift from God? If the key issue is to find the relationship that God has made possible, then the practical question is how does this play out in the pastoral relationship. It is through prospecting for the signs of grace in human life.

Part I: History, Framework, and Theology

A friend, who recently saw again the film *Les Miserables*, was so surprised when the key scene at the church brought him to tears once more. Jean Valjean is arrested by Inspector Javert, a thief caught red-handed carrying a chalice from a church altar. As Jean is about to be dragged away, Bishop Myriel comes rushing down the steps of the church toward them holding two candlesticks, exclaiming, "Why did you forget these, they were part of the gift as well." Jean is astonished and the legalistic inspector furious. This act of the bishop is much more than forgiving Jean, this act places the whole episode in an entirely new context. This moment was to stay with Jean for the rest of his life. This act of grace, recontextualizes the whole event, leaving Jean free and the inspector's accusations groundless. Jean does nothing, this happens to him. Most commentators describe this as an act of forgiveness by the bishop, but it is far more than that. Victor Hugo has grasped in some fashion what the Apostle Paul discovered and called grace.

Paul's experience on the road to Damascus confounds him. Afterward he knows that what has happened is so momentous, that he has to reach for a new language which is so much more than a restoration which includes the forgiveness of sins. He reconfigures the accepted understanding of God's coming apocalyptic judgment of the world. In Paul's time there were many writers providing a timeline for the events of a coming catastrophic apocalypse when finally God would step into human history and bring God's ultimate judgment upon the terrible injustice wrought by dictators and their empires throughout human history.

What he discovers is that this future apocalypse has already happened in the life, death, resurrection, and ascension of Jesus Christ. It was an apocalypse of Jesus Christ. (In Gal 1:12, the original Greek has an apocalypse of Jesus Christ, whereas translations since AD 400 replace apocalypse with revelation.)[5] These events disclose that God has already acted in human history in a way far beyond expectation, recontextualizing all life in terms of Jesus Christ. In him God had already brought into being a new creation, a cosmic context for grace.

This places (recontextualizes) all relationships in a new setting, that of a reconciled creation. The rest of his life was spent focused on making known that already the human race is open to a God-generated, God-given relationship with each other within the creation. CPE is faced with the reality of the total relationship within which the visitor and the visited is

---

5. Drayton, *Apocalyptic Good News*, 28–30.

found. It is not about helping an individual in need to embark on a therapeutic process, whether in terms of a deepening relationship, the finding of a purpose in life, or the importance of spiritual practices. It is about the visitor and the visited finding God's way of acting, rather than the visitor helping the visited on a spiritually therapeutic process. It starts with God and involves them both, visitor and visited, rather than starting with the individual and leading toward God's action.

The limiting of the message within a God and me framework limits this relationship to a one way person to God exploration, and is not able to address the vast inter-related network of relationships when the relationship begins with God and incorporates the redemptive restoration of creation.

God's action toward the creation immerses all things in a host of other interdependent relationships. This flow from God is a multi-linked and multi inter-related matrix of links made evident in the apocalyptic event of the cross.

> For in him the fullness of God was pleased to dwell, and through him God was pleased to reconcile to God all things, whether on earth or in heaven, by making peace through the blood of the cross. (Col 1:19–20)

Two individuals speaking together in a room are but part of the reconciliation of God to *all things* that happened in the cross.

That reconciliation has important ramifications for the one on one meeting of the pastoral relationship. Paul speaks of God's reconciliation with the world and implores all who hear to respond to this by being reconciled to Christ. In the prevenient work of the Holy Spirit, God is present in some way to the person visited. This provides another perspective to Pattison's claim that the Bible is silent about the nature of this relationship. God is already at work in the life of the visited person whether they are yet aware of it or not. Jesus in his declaration of the kingdom of God in the parable of the sower speaks of the word of God being broadcast over all. He that has ears to hear, let him listen. This seed of the kingdom of God brings the possibility of new life in the realm of the Spirit, especially for those who find themselves in the midst of crises, times of reassessment, uncertainty about the future, dark times, threats to life itself.

Of course, it is helpful to point a person toward this spiritual reality where possible, but that is limited and constrained within the boundaries of a one on one pastoral conversation.

The pastoral visitor however is quite free to ask questions that are part of the broad gamut involved in sharing during a visit. Active and creative listening involves the use of the questions of what, how, why, when, who, and more particular questions that leave the person free to respond or not are helpful. Questions like:

- What are the most profound moments and events in your life that have happened to you?
- What has happened to you that you will never forget?

PROSPECTING FOR GRACE

It is important to emphasise that the visitor is working with clear boundaries that are to be respected, acknowledging the rights and integrity of visitor and visited. This setting is not under any circumstance an occasion for the visitor to try to share a new perspective, argue that the general understanding of forgiveness is flawed, or discredit what the person thinks needs to happen. That would change the dynamics of the visit from a relationship of presence to one of having to impart information, persuade another, or even seek to convert them to a new way of thinking and experiencing.

This zone of discovery, however, is one in which the full range of language and experience can be explored to search out the moments of grace that have bubbled up, or brought stark realization, or deep peace and assurance in the midst of life. The pastoral visitor comes to this sort of conversation with usually a greater awareness of the way the spirit of God is at work in human life, and may well be able to hear how the Spirit is involved in the life of the person visited.

Such moments and events leave a trace that is not forgotten, for there is a quality of life, truth, and love in them that is alive and real. This is the way eternal life is given by the Holy Spirit as she breathes and blows through life to all life. If in conversation it is possible to re-awaken these times in either, or both, the visitor and visited then a new framework is available for discussion. The realization and sharing of even limited moments brings the possibility of the greater promise of further experiences of grace.

There is no template for such conversations. It is like prospecting for that which may or may not be there. It is a form of listening and recognition that resets the relationship and the discussion. It would be helpful to list many examples of this happening. It is a start to have here two quite different examples, the first opening an experience of intense life, the second involving a puzzled query that brought peace.

He was not really interested in spiritual things, and steered the conversation away from religious stuff. So we talked about his life, his hopes and dreams. I must have asked him what he did for relaxation. "I can't wait for the times when I get my rod and head off up-river to catch salmon," he said, the tone of his voice changing. "I love fly fishing. I enjoy standing in my waders for hours, just being there in the river. But I live for that moment when a salmon strikes. It comes out of the blue. The thrill of the struggle is . . ." (he couldn't find the word to encompass what he wanted to say—something like profound, I think). He knew all about the thrill of life, the finding of treasure. And he was talking to a line fisher. The conversation moved into another realm of the flashes of intense life. We then had an entrée into sharing about that which is most precious in life, the grace of moments unbidden which change everything.

An Australian woman had a car accident on Highway 66 in Illinois, in the United States. She found herself unexpectedly in hospital, bruised and alone. The nursing staff knew of me, an Australian minister serving a congregation nearby. Could I come and see her? "Of course!" I found her room overlooking a ploughed field and a row of trees in the wintry sun of the late afternoon. We said our hellos and she shared a bit of the day's crisis. Then she stopped and said, "Can I ask you a question?" When I said yes, she pointed to one of the trees about a hundred meters away. "That tree, and only that tree, has been glowing more than any of the trees around it for the last fifteen minutes. The glow then gradually faded and now it is like the others. What is happening?" I remember stopping in surprise, caught by this change in the direction of the conversation and was unsure what to say. Then the thought came, "How did you feel looking at the tree." She said, "A deep, deep peace, that despite today all will work out OK." I found myself saying, "Perhaps it was a gift from God to reassure you." And the conversation went on from there.

The characteristic of these events is that they happen to us. It may be a dream, a telling phrase, a sunset, an argument, a moment in a song, a word of affirmation, a voice in our head, a thought, a journey, a miracle, a meeting, a light in the darkness. . . . It is not something that we do or create—these events find us.

Part I: History, Framework, and Theology

IMPLICATIONS FOR PASTORAL VISITATION

What does this mean for pastoral visitation? The great gift of pastoral sharing through clinical pastoral education, is to create the space for lives to be shared through visitation. In more technical terms it is a respectful exploration of the case history of the person being visited. What is vital is the ability to listen creatively and actively for the sort of life determining events that this person has had.

In this prospecting for grace, it is being alive to such events in life that are seeds of the kingdom of God/heaven, the touch of the Spirit of God. They are not necessarily religious. The listening opens the possibility to discover the grace within these occasions. The gospel is that God is always present to us, known or not, recognized or not. In the visit it may be possible to find the particular and surprising ways that God has blessed and blesses our lives.

This sort of sharing is not alien to CPE. In fact CPE training is vital in helping develop the skill of active and creative listening. The prospector never knows what is present until the searching has happened. In the pastoral setting, the ears are on high alert for events that have been pivotal in the life of the person visited, and the corresponding echoes in the visitor's life.

This listening is much more than a therapeutic process. This listening is about identifying the traces of God's Spirit in a human life. It is the prospecting for grace, like prospecting for water, or using a metal detector to find coins. Listening, walking respectfully across the landscape of life, listening for the sign of something when at first there is nothing to be heard.

Such a conversation embodies a fundamental respect for the experience of the other as the source of that which has blessed them and encouraged them. Such times are an opening to the reality of the divine presence already known, no matter in how limited or great a way. Such an opening allows all of creation to be brought into the conversation. The God of creation and redemption has been given space for the grace of God to be at work. What was understood to be an exploration of the therapeutic nature of the relationship opens up to a way of exploring the graceful source of all life. This exploration goes beyond an aim of a person discovering spiritual resources for their own healing, as important as that may be, to find the spiritual resources God has for them.

CONCLUSION

An exploration of worldview assumptions highlights the limitations that the highly individualized nature of contemporary religious life has placed on the practice of clinical pastoral education. As the sharing has indicated, the *me and God* world that most inhabit has limited the possibility for understanding and experiencing the redemption of the creation that is at the heart of the mission of God. This prospecting for grace, finding the seeds of the kingdom of God/heaven, has been applied within the particular constraints that CPE works, namely being faithful to religious discourse in a secular world. It is not meant to downgrade efforts to provide a therapeutic approach, but seeks to place this practice in a more inclusive theological framework of God's move to redeem the creation that can be discovered in the constraints of the one-to-one context of a pastoral visit.

BIBLIOGRAPHY

Drayton, R. Dean. *Apocalyptic Good News: Christ in the Cosmos*. Eugene, OR: Wipf & Stock, 2019.

Holifield, E. Brooks. *A History of Pastoral Care in America: From Salvation to Self-Realization*. Nashville: Abingdon, 1983.

Pattison, Stephen. *A Critique of Pastoral Care*. London: SCM, 1988.

Reiff, Philip. *The Triumph of the Therapeutic: Uses of Faith after Freud*. Boston: InterCollegiate, 2006.

PART II

CLINICAL PASTORAL EDUCATION AND SPIRITUAL PRACTICE IN A SECULAR WORLD

5

Black Fella CPE

Supervision in an Australian Indigenous Community

PETER POWELL

BEGINNINGS

THE REQUEST FOR AN introductory CPE program in northern New South Wales came from members of an Aboriginal Christian Community. The contact came about through my relationship with workers connected to other Indigenous communities.

INITIAL CHALLENGES

The group had a long-term relationship with a local Anglo congregation, which was beginning to fracture. There were different cultural views about the use of space in a hall. The Aboriginal community felt rejected by those representing a culture under which they had felt oppressed. Most of the group members came from families of disposition, stolen generation and a variety of experiences of racism.[1] In addition, the educational community within which I was working was itself enmeshed within a complex web

---

1. Bodkin-Andrews and Carlson, "Legacy of Racism."

of social deprivation. The almost inevitable severe mental health implications were clear to see in the wider community, both Indigenous and non-Indigenous peoples.[2]

DEVELOPING ACCEPTANCE: LISTENING AND USE OF LANGUAGE

Despite the background of abuse suffered by many of the participants, they were open and inclusive of me as an Anglo-Australian, or white fella, to the point of referring to me as one of the mob. This language of inclusion relied significantly on the fact that I listened respectfully to their stories. Recent research has consistently demonstrated how language shapes the way people think and behave.[3] In various workplaces, churches, and other social settings, the use of language that is respectful, inclusive, non-sexist and non-racist has become the norm.

> Language pervades social life. It is the principle vehicle for the transmission of cultural knowledge, and the primary means by which we gain access to the contents of others minds.[4]

The way we use language communicates to others what we think of them and how we construct our view of relationships. Language is a core element in human interaction and can have a profound effect on how people perceive interpersonal interactions; consequently, developing positive relationships relies on the use of language that is respectful and invites other people into relational spaces where they feel valued.

> Language is implicated in most of the phenomena that lie at the core of social psychology: attitude change, social perception, personal identity, social interaction, intergroup bias and stereotyping, attribution and so on.[5]

---

2. Hunter, "Disadvantage and Discontent."
3. Boroditsky, "How Language Shapes Thought."
4. Krauss and Chiu, "Language and Social Behaviour," 41.
5. Krauss and Chiu, "Language and Social Behaviour," 41.

LANGUAGE AND STORY: THE WAY OF NOT KNOWING

I see language as a broader process than merely words used. It includes every aspect of the complex ways in which people communicate to and with each other, including attitudes, body language, and facial expressions. Communication is a complex process, precisely because people hear the same information and process it in their own unique ways, thus creating a myriad of meanings, as well as misunderstandings.

In the educational process with the Aboriginal community, language included conducting the learning in particular places of safety for the community, as well as being willing to meet and spend time with wider members of the community. The neatness of boundaries that might otherwise guide a Western analytically influenced learning group was not useful in a community where the connections were more complex and fluid. While it is important not to violate boundaries—such as taking financial advantage of clients—there is sometimes a requirement to cross boundaries for the benefit of clients; such as walking outside with an agoraphobic client.[6] As much of the work done by my students involved social justice, I met family members, clients of the Aboriginal workers, and Family and Community Services staff and wrote letters to members of parliament. I explored each boundary crossing carefully before taking action. The following quote refers to therapy; however, the principles remain the same for supervision.

> Boundary crossings should be implemented according to the client's unique situation, condition, problems, personality, culture, and history and the setting in which therapy takes place. The rationale of boundary crossing, like any therapeutic intervention, should be articulated (in writing) in the treatment plan and consultations with experts are advised in complex cases. The unduly restrictive analytic risk-management emphasis on clearly defined, rigid, and inflexible boundaries often interferes with sound clinical judgment, which ought to be flexible and personally tailored to clients' needs rather than to therapists' dogmas or fears.[7]

As supervisor, I was still seen in a particular teaching role in relationship with the group; however, as the group developed over time, I moved from being referred to hierarchically as Dr. Powell, then more familiarly as Dr. Peter and then to Uncle, a most prestigious position of honour and respect.

---

6. Zur, "To Cross or Not to Cross."
7. Zur, "To Cross or Not to Cross."

Eventually, the community members asked if I would accept a Bundjalung name. So it was that I became Bana Gali Bygal, literally *strong man*.

Within another culture the story may develop differently, but it is always the wisdom contained in the story that reveals the most effective supervisory process.

LANGUAGE AND STORY: CULTURAL DOMINANCE OR RELATIONAL COMMUNITY

The language people use creates the stories within which they live. Those stories, in turn, create and shape the culture in which they give allegiance. Once allegiance is given to the cultural story, it tends to be the one that will dominate a person's thinking. Herein lies a social risk. When cultural stories are open to other stories, creative intercultural dialogue is possible, leading to enriched societies. However, if cultural stories exclude other stories, they create the essence of literal fundamentalism in all its forms. This has implications for CPE supervision.

CPE supervisors and those they supervise need to put aside the desire to grasp ultimate knowledge, so that they can learn the strategies that will be effective in supervision and providing care for others. This requires a letting go of any attempt to understand the story of the other, in order that the story of the other teaches its meeting. Herein, we discover a dilemma. The desire to know and conquer ignorance is built into the human struggle for existence. We want to understand, not only to work out the meaning of whatever situation in which we are involved, but also to reduce the anxiety of not knowing; consequently, avoiding the shame of ignorance.[8] The Hebrew story of human rebellion in the garden of Eden, in Genesis 3, provides a way to clarify this issue, where the challenge for humankind is whether to seek the certainty of knowledge, or to live by faith in relationship with others and by faith with the Divine.

Maslow adds further weight to the argument by suggesting that the need to gain knowledge about people can often be anxiety instigated, thus constituting a cognitive pathology:

> When the need to know is based on the compulsive seeking after certainty rather than on enjoyment of discovery, it is pathological.[9]

---

8. Powell, *Story Wisdom*, 6.
9. Sollod and Monte, *Beneath the Mask*, 418.

Peter Powell | Black Fella CPE

STORY: TRUE OR FALSE?

I propose that all stories are true and that the narrative cannot lie. Stories need to be given space to be told and treated with deep respect. When the story is allowed to sit in creative dialogue with the story of the other, both personal and communal, it always leads to a functional outcome, even when the story being told is antisocial. Either the story will teach the person that they need to change, or the story will continue to be told in a way that does not lead to change. The latter story reveals what in psychological terms would be called a narcissistic personality, where people are unable to develop empathy for others and experience grace. Either way, the story is a true revealing of a person's life.

It follows then that we need to be concerned less about a search for truth about a person's story and pay more attention to the stories themselves, regardless of their source. If the story being told is clearly antisocial and against the creative purpose of human relationships, it will either be reframed and told differently (repentance leading to positive change) or retold in the same dysfunctional way, with little insight or desire for change.

I spent considerable time listening to the stories told by members of the Aboriginal community. I was aware, very early on, that the experience of listening to stories of cultural destruction imposed over many years, was a completely different experience to reading research about such experiences. I voted in 1967 for Aboriginal people to be included in the national census; that is, counted as part of a population and no longer described as *flora and fauna*, thinking at the time that I was a culturally informed person. Sitting within the story, receiving information first hand, was a different and painful experience.

As I spent significant time building trust in relationships, I could hear ringing in my ears a statement I heard from a Tongan theologian: "If the sacred text of the Bible clashes with culture, abandon the text!" As a result, I needed to hear stories told through the lens of 220 years of cultural abuse, of stolen children, slavery, murder, rape, poisoned wells, economic exploitation, and denial of Indigenous language. Thus, the Christian story emerging from the life of Jesus—where justice and compassion for the poor and abused is central—took on a completely different meaning, as did the texts that related to those stories past and present.

Part II: Clinical Pastoral Education and Spiritual Practice

UNFOLDING CHALLENGES

Literacy

All participants received a handbook that outlined the requirements of the New South Wales College of Clinical Pastoral Education (NSWCCPE), with some adaptations of language to adjust for the group, where there was some significant literacy difficulty.

Significant adjustments had to be made so that participants could prepare material for learning; particularly, where students could not read or write. In one case, a student could speak fluent Bundjalung and English, but could not read or write in either language.

Cultural Identity

One participant had a Bundjalung mother and a father from Vanuatu who had been kidnapped for the cane farming in Queensland. Not only did he have those issues of abuse to integrate, he also had to endure the racial taunts from some Aboriginal people who saw him as a foreigner. Most participants had abuse backgrounds of stolen generation families, generational disposition and dysfunction. While the dominant group was Bundjalung, there were also marriages with partners from Vanuatu and Fiji.

Group Structure

Determining the numbers to participate was a key question. There is a minimum recommendation in the New South Wales (NSW) CPE regulations of six students for a forty-hour unit of CPE. There is no upper limit for forty-hour introductory CPE; however, educational principles still need to guide the decision. I based my criteria on what would enable this community to learn well together, as well as in a way that would strengthen community bonds. So many times in the past, white fella interventions, no matter how well-meaning, have created poor learning outcomes. The group initially began with seven members.

Group Identity

One key reason I propose for previous poor learning outcomes is the power differential between teacher and learner, as well as the discounting of the contribution of Aboriginal communities toward their own learning. For long periods of time, Aboriginal people were prohibited from speaking in their own languages, or celebrating their own customs. Education for Aboriginal people was built around patronizing processes and the insensitivity of the dominant culture.[10] This at times has led to cargo cult thinking among Aboriginal peoples.[11] This issue showed up even before the program began. The coordinator said to me, "We need the certificate." When becoming curious about the meaning of this statement, I learned that this community had lived for so many generations as a discounted and dispossessed community, that they saw gaining the white fella's certificate as one way to gain credibility for the ministry they were already undertaking. While providing some quite radical, supportive ministry to very troubled individuals and families, there was little recognition from some white fella professionals for what the Aboriginal workers were doing: as they were "not qualified." Thus, given the wisdom revealed through the cultural story, I decided to work with the tension between learning with an open-ended outcome and one that was more focused on a culturally-driven goal. I negotiated this issue to be part of the action-reflection learning process.

Group Process

It did not take long for underlying tensions within the Aboriginal community to emerge, some of which also showed up in the learning group. Attachment and identity formation has always been integral to the pastoral and psychological work I do; in this community, it was even more critical. I identified the following issues early on:

1. No formal theological, psychological or pastoral education; as well as little general schooling upon which to build learning.
2. No formal administrative/accountability structure.
3. Pastoral leadership emerging by consensus, sometimes linked to the role of Aunty and Uncle.

10. Bodkin-Andrews and Carlson, "Legacy of Racism"; Hogarth, "Critical Analysis."
11. Worsley, "50 Years Ago."

4. Identity confused by conflicting loyalties to nation, family, tradition, and Christian dogma.

5. Varying levels of literacy with some leaders unable to read and write English or their native tongue but orally fluent in the recovered language of origin.

6. High levels of social chaos, including alcohol and other drug abuse, drug trafficking, a wide variety of petty criminal behavior, homelessness, domestic violence, child sexual abuse, removal of children, marital and family breakdown, unemployment, and a variety of types of mental illness.

OUTCOMES

Literacy

Given the difficulties with literacy, I made significant adaptations to the requirements of the CPE College, such as written verbatims and theological position papers. Some chose to dictate to others typing up the notes, even then, presentations were sometimes difficult to read.

Other methods included oral story-telling, use of symbols, examining family systems and using multi-generational genograms. I chose to use multiple forms of communication and a wide range of literary forms beyond writing.

Cultural Identity

For many years, I have centered my psychological and pastoral practice around issues of attachment and identity. I am firmly convinced by the evidence, that a clear positive sense of identity becomes critical for a whole range of personal and societal attitudes and behaviors. The destruction of much of the cultural fabric of the members of the group I was instructing severely impacted their learning. Members would move from submissiveness to the white fella's authority, through to pushback against academic requirements. I saw it is critical to bring that part of the story into the dynamic of what we were processing. I asked such questions as, "Who are you?"; "In this pastoral situation something is going on that makes it difficult for you to listen, I would love to clarify more?"; "I'm interested to know how this aspect of the visit with that person affected you as a pastoral person?"; "I wonder how the government department's response angered the patient?"

It is in situations such as this that the creative tension between supervision and therapy comes into play. While I kept the focus on the supervision issues around providing pastoral care into the community, therapeutic issues were a constant presence.[12] As members of the learning group developed a stronger cultural and personal awareness, as well as identity, they became aware that their next major task was facilitating a similar process within the Aboriginal community. This led to the establishment of an introductory CPE program, where previous graduates invited appropriate Aboriginal persons to participate. The intent of the program was to focus on identity development in the context of pastoral care delivery. The participants came from backgrounds of stolen generation, social deprivation, times in prison, as well as recovery from alcohol and other drug abuse.

Group Structure

The group consisted of three couples and one single female. The group meetings were a combination of online videoconferencing and face-to-face on site. After the first three-day intensive, one of the members gained employment, making it impossible to attend the intensives during the week. The group discussed the matter and agreed to extend the program over weekend intensives. The newly employed person was quite moved by the willingness of his peer group to adjust their schedules. At the next intensive the employed man and his wife did not arrive. They informed the coordinator at the last minute that they could not leave their house, as there were other Aboriginal persons rioting outside the house, accusing their son of stealing drugs. I arranged for them to do some reflection on that experience, and the ministry they could, or could not provide in that situation. This reflection was never completed.

At the next intensive the couple failed to arrive again. I was informed that there was a major land rights meeting in the Northern Territory to which they had been invited. I was excited for them to have this opportunity, and also aware that they had chosen that activity in preference to the contract made with the learning group. In addition, they made no contact with me to explain the change. While the Aboriginal coordinator was

12. Powell, "Being in Tune."

irritated by this "rudeness," it was also common within the cultural group for such actions to be taken.

Group Process and Identity

It soon became clear that the absent couple were less concerned about the training and accreditation than the remainder of the group, particularly when there were other cultural issues to be addressed by them.

The group continued with the five remaining members. Tension arose between the coordinating couple and the other couple over the way the husband related to his wife. He was controlling in a quiet and calm way. When that was pointed out by other members of the group he got defensive and denied he behaved in that way. His explanation was that he was protecting his wife. After other members of the group had raised the issue, his wife had the courage to confirm what the others were saying and to speak directly to him. She later told one of the women in the group later on, that as soon as she got home she fell back into a submissive role.

Two-thirds into the group process the issue sparked again, leading to a loud verbal exchange between the two males. Unfortunately, this was one of the online intensives and I was six hundred kilometers away. It was very difficult to facilitate the tense interaction, and finally the man being challenged about his behavior stormed out of the room, taking his wife with him. They did not return to the training group or respond to my phone calls or texts. I learned later on that the wife had indicated fear within the relationship to others, but was uncertain how to proceed.

The group concluded with the remaining three members. All group members, including the couple that left, were diligent in presenting case material for individual and group supervision.

SUMMARY

I cannot cover all issues in this brief chapter; however, a number of learning issues emerged:

1. It is possible to supervise a group from a different cultural and social background to the supervisor, provided the supervisor is intentional about the narrative of the learning group.

2. Learning can be successfully facilitated online; however, when critical issues such as conflict arise it can make the process more difficult.

3. Awareness of the dominant cultural narratives and a willingness to be creative and adaptable becomes critical when working in cross-cultural environments.

4. Supervisors need to be able to work within a certain level of chaos, as multiple learning, family, personal, and cultural issues clash.

5. Supervisors need to be very clear about their own personal identity and aware of any remaining attachment anxiety.

6. It is possible for a culturally deprived and abused group to use CPE to develop a sense of identity and to shape CPE into a form unique to that group; that is, Black Fella CPE.

7. The basic principles of boundaries still apply; however, the way boundaries are applied will appear very different to a CPE group in a White Fella situation.

BIBLIOGRAPHY

Bodkin-Andrews, G., and Bronwyn Carlson. "The Legacy of Racism and Indigenous Australian Identity within Education." *Race, Ethnicity and Education* 19 (2016) 784–807.

Boroditsky, Lera. "How Language Shapes Thought." *Scientific American* 304 (2011) 63–65.

Hogarth, Melitta D. "A Critical Analysis of the Aboriginal and Torres Straight Islander Education Action Plan." Master's thesis, Queensland University of Technology, 2015.

Hunter, Ernest. "Disadvantage and Discontent: A Review of the Issues Relevant to the Mental Health of Rural and Remote Indigenous Australians." *Australian Journal of Rural Health* 15 (2007) 88–93.

Krauss, Robert M., and Chi-Yue Chiu. "Language and Social Behaviour." In *Handbook of Social Psychology*, edited by Daniel T. Gilbert et al., 41–88. 4th ed. Boston: McGraw-Hill, 2010.

Powell, Peter. "Being in Tune in Clinical Pastoral Education: Supervision or Therapy." Paper presented at the Australian & New Zealand Association of Clinical Pastoral Education Conference, Adelaide, Australia, 2019.

———. *Story Wisdom: An Introduction to Biblical-Narrative Therapy*. North Parramatta, Australia: Pastoral Counselling Institute, 2019.

Sollod, Robert N., and Christopher F. Monte. *Beneath the Mask: An Introduction to Theories of Personality*. 8th ed. Hoboken, NJ: Wiley, 2009.

Watters, Ethan. *Crazy Like Us: The Globalization of the American Psyche*. New York: Free Press, 2010.

Part II: Clinical Pastoral Education and Spiritual Practice

Worsley, Peter M. "50 Years Ago: Cargo Cults of Melanesia." *Scientific American*, May 1, 2009. https://www.scientificamerican.com/article/1959-cargo-cults-melanesia/.

Zur, Ofer. "To Cross or Not to Cross: Do Boundaries in Therapy Protect or Harm?" *Psychotherapy Bulletin* 39 (2018) 27–32.

6

The Challenge of Supervising Evangelical Clinical Pastoral Education Trainees in Sydney, Australia

Morris Sing Key

FOR TWENTY YEARS (1994–2014) I was the preferred CPE supervisor for many of the Evangelical CPE trainees from both the Presbyterian and Anglican Churches in Sydney, Australia. In that period of time, I noticed a number of characteristics among my evangelical CPE trainees which became very clear and evident.

Over the past twenty years I have come across a number of pastoral care and spiritual assessment models that I have liked and modified and adapted for use in my supervision of Evangelical CPE trainees. The why, how, and when are seamlessly built into these models.

Some of the models that I have found to be helpful in my supervision of such trainees are:

1. The Seven Functions of Pastoral Care.

2. The VDI Model: Ventilation, Differentiation, and Integration.

3. The Drama Triangle.

Part II: Clinical Pastoral Education and Spiritual Practice

4. The Fitchett 7 x 7 Spiritual Assessment Model.

I realize that while there are certain advantages of using and adapting these models for supervision, there are also disadvantages that need to be considered. Pastoral care and spiritual assessment models have the effect of lowering the anxiety of these trainees and this can be very helpful for their ministry. However, there is a downside to the use of these models. There is the real danger that trainees may get too caught up with the models and analyze and objectify the patient rather than just being with where the patient is emotionally and being able to listen and respond with empathy and generally offer pastoral care to the patient.

In my experience of supervising such trainees I have discovered that there are four characteristic features common to evangelical CPE trainees.

FOUR CHARACTERISTIC FEATURES OF AN EVANGELICAL TRAINEE (ET)

1. ETs Are Wary and Sometimes Resistant to the Process of CPE

Historically, many such trainees who have done CPE have had rather painful and negative experiences of CPE. In the past, they have had CPE supervisors and even chaplaincy departments tell them that evangelism and sharing the gospel is forbidden. This has caused some of them to hide their true selves and to be very selective when they present their verbatim material to their CPE supervisors. Some trainees almost have a siege mentality rationalizing their experience as "the faithful versus the world."

2. An ET's Agenda or Need is to Share the Gospel or to Evangelize the Patient

Evangelical trainees generally feel a great need to be faithful to the great commission of going into the world, to share the good news of Jesus Christ. The theology of the evangelical trainees and their practice of this theology fits the framework of Fitchett's 7 x 7 Spiritual Assessment model, which consist of Beliefs and Meaning.[1] The evangelical trainee's theology is their beliefs and meaning. Their belief is that people need a savior and that Jesus Christ is the only way. The only way that these people are going to hear this good news is if they share the gospel with them. Fitchett's *Vocation*

---

1 Fitchett, *Assessing Spiritual Needs*, 45.

and Consequence[2] (these are the duties and obligations that a person feels called to fulfill, a direct consequence of a person's beliefs and meaning) thus becomes the evangelical trainee's agenda and need to share the gospel.

3. ETs Need to Defend or Rescue God, the Authority of the Bible, the Church, or Their Theology

The *Authority and Guidance*[3] for most evangelical trainees is the Bible and their understanding and interpretation of it. They seem to have a great need to defend God, the authority of the bible, the church or their theology if these are under attack or being questioned.

4. ETs Have Difficulty Recognizing Feelings and Usually Respond with Their Intellect

I know that this difficulty is not the exclusive domain of evangelical CPE trainees, but many such trainees respond from the "head" or intellect and struggle to connect emotionally with patients. So the big challenge remains: How does one supervise Evangelical CPE trainees?

WHAT ARE SOME OF MY SUPERVISORY STRATEGIES FOR SUCH TRAINEES?

1. Provide a Safe Place for Evangelical Trainees to Learn and to Grow

I am convinced that these highly anxious trainees need to feel safe and have their theology understood before they will be able and willing to explore new ways of ministering to people. If they feel that their theology and the way they express or practice it, is frowned upon or disliked or even under attack, then there will be resentment and resistance to new learning and they will be selective in what clinical materials and verbatims they are willing to present to their supervisor.

An understanding of this background is important because many evangelical trainees coming to do CPE usually measure their effectiveness in hospital chaplaincy by the number of times they were able to share the

---

2. Fitchett, *Assessing Spiritual Needs*, 46.
3. Fitchett, *Assessing Spiritual Needs*, 49.

gospel in a hospital context. Here, it is hoped that such trainees will come to appreciate and to understand more of the Ministry of the Presence rather than just the Ministry of the Word.

The Challenges That Faced Me as a CPE Supervisor Are:

1. How do I allow such trainees to hold onto their theology and passion to share the gospel and yet at the same time, protect vulnerable patients from potential spiritual and pastoral abuse or what I have called evangelism? (Vandalizing evangelism).

2. A second challenge is the realization that many evangelical trainees have great trouble with listening to patients and responding with empathy. It seems like they respond from the "head" and have a real struggle and difficulty coming up with feeling words.

3. A third challenge is that they find it difficult not to become defensive if patients make critical comments about the church or God or express a different theology to theirs. They tend to rush in and want to rescue or defend what is under attack.

Emmanuel Y. Lartey in his book *In Living Color* talks about the seven functions of pastoral care: healing, guiding, sustaining, reconciling, nurturing, liberating, and empowerment.[4]

When evangelical CPE trainees become familiar with the seven functions of pastoral care, many of them feel relieved and liberated as they realize that there can be a legitimate place for them to share the gospel with patients within the pastoral care framework under the pastoral care function of "reconciliation" by reconciling a patient to God.

One particular evangelical CPE trainee said after being introduced to this model in her very first CPE unit, "This makes all the difference. I feel so relieved that I don't have to feel guilty if I don't share the gospel every time I visit a patient."

The great advantage of these seven functions of pastoral care is that it gives the evangelical trainee a much wider range of pastoral care options

---

4. Lartey, *Living Color*, 60–78. Author Emmanuel Y. Lartey talks of empowerment as the seventh function of pastoral care; healing, guiding, and sustaining is from Hiltner, *Preface to Pastoral Theology*, 89–174; reconciling is from Clebsch and Jaekle, *Pastoral Care*, 56–66; nurturing is from Clinebell, *Basic Types*, 42–43; liberating is from Lester, *Hope in Pastoral Care & Counseling*, introductory page.

and it also makes them aware of the important pastoral and supervisory issue of *Whose need is being met?* at the time.

This meets the *why* (the rationale) of introducing this pastoral function framework to them. The *how* (the methodology) and the *when* (timing) is usually when the verbatim material of the trainee is suitable for the advantages of this pastoral framework to be illustrated.

In just about every unit of CPE with ETs, this issue of *whose need is being met* comes up when a trainee's agenda differs from that of a patient. My supervisory stance in such a situation *is to focus on the patient* and to help the trainee to ask . . . how did the patient present themselves, what did they choose to share with you (stories, feelings, etc.) and what did they think the main pastoral care need of the patient was?

When ETs discover that a patient needed sustaining because they were feeling so overwhelmed rather than reconciling (the trainee's need and attempt to share the gospel), they become more open to the broader pastoral care framework and option. The *focus on the patient, their feelings and the pastoral care need of the patient* is important as it shifts the spotlight away from the trainee's attempts, lowers their anxiety levels and allows them to entertain alternative ways to minister to patients.[5]

When this emphasis is explored in the group or even in an individual session, trainees begin to realize that when their agendas or needs override those of the patient, good pastoral care is sabotaged and effective listening almost impossible to achieve. This is where Fitchett's *courage and growth* dimension comes in,[6] and the trainees may need to have the courage to reject as inadequate their previous way of ministering to patients and be more open to the growth of embracing and attempting new ways of ministering more effectively to patients.

2. Broaden the Spiritual Assessment Approach of Evangelical Trainees

I can still remember the visit of Professor George Fitchett to Sydney some years ago and his introduction to his 7 x 7 Spiritual Assessment model. Some CPE supervisors took this model of spiritual assessment and incorporated it into their programs whilst others seemed ambivalent about using this model at all. I was trained at the Royal North Shore Hospital CPE

---

5. Hawkins and Shohet, *Supervision in Helping Professions*, 56, 59–60. Modified version of mode one of their process model.

6. Fitchett, *Assessing Spiritual Needs*, 48.

Centre and this model of spiritual assessment was included as part of my supervisory training.

Whether they are consciously aware of it or not, evangelically minded trainees are constantly making spiritual assessments of their patients. They however, use a *substantive*[7] approach of spiritual assessment which *focuses on whether a patient holds certain specific beliefs about God or Jesus Christ or about sin or the gospel or the church* to determine whether a patient fits their description or definition or understanding of a Christian.

The Fitchett 7 x 7 Model of spiritual assessment employs a different approach which is a *functional* approach. This approach focuses more on *how* a person makes meaning and purpose in their lives rather than on *what* that specific meaning is.[8]

The advantage of the Fitchett spiritual assessment model is that it can help the trainee to see the limitations of their single dimensional approach of *just* assessing people from the beliefs they may hold. When such trainees understand the 7 x 7 model a little better, they may be able to realize the significant role that culture, family, personality, and health play in the spiritual formation of patients.

This is my rational (why) for introducing this model to the trainees. Trainees differ in their ability to see the relevance and the need of this spiritual assessment model. Some take to this model like a duck to water whereas others use it sparingly. I usually model the use of this assessment approach whenever it is appropriate and even then, only highlight only one or two of the seven spiritual dimensions that are obvious in the verbatim (the *how* and *when*).

The Fitchett model has stimulated my own thoughts as I work with evangelical trainees. I have discovered that within this model there can be a new way of understanding what is being said by the patient which has the potential to change the way evangelical trainees hear and respond to patients.

This is especially in the case when patients are critical about the church, God or Christianity and such trainees feel a great need to defend or to rescue the church, God, or Christianity. Here I focus on just three of the seven spiritual dimensions of the Fitchett 7 x 7 model, *Belief and Meaning*, *Emotion and Experience*, and *Courage and Growth*, and show how they can change the way we hear and respond.

7. Fitchett, *Assessing Spiritual Needs*, 40.
8. Fitchett, *Assessing Spiritual Needs*, 40.

It is my firm belief that most of us develop our beliefs and meaning about God, church, or Christianity during the good times. When something bad has happened in their past life some people may well question the goodness or the love of God. People usually respond in two ways.

First, their beliefs and meaning (that *God is good*) may be sorely tested because of their past emotion and experience. However their beliefs and meaning may be strengthened and deepened and Bible verses from the scriptures become not just well-known verses, but verses real and tried and tested and proven through events in life. God is hence still good and loving despite their bad or negative experiences and emotions.

But for some other people, their beliefs and meaning may just collapse as their emotion and experience (bad) seem to totally contradict their previous beliefs and meaning (that God is good). For them, God may now be experienced as *cruel and unloving*. This is a new beliefs and meaning and they may well have many unanswered *why* questions.

People whose beliefs and meaning no longer *fit* their present emotion and experience will need *courage and growth* (Fitchett) to develop a new beliefs and meaning that more accurately fits their present circumstances.[9]

What is important for ETs to recognize is that when patients yell and scream and make negative statements about God or the church or Christianity they are also making a statement of their previous experiences and emotions about God or the church or perhaps one of God's representatives. If ETs can recognize this, it may give them a different way of hearing and responding to a patient's pain and ventilation.

Antony F. Krisak suggests that a better way to do ministry is to focus on process rather than content.[10] According to Krisak, when a person focuses on the *content* of a patient expressing grief, *debate and apology take over*.

Avoiding this path entails making an important distinction between what is said and what is meant. *This distinction changes the way the chaplains respond.* Focus on the process of a patient expressing grief creates an opportunity for the trainee and the patient to explore the emotional component of the grief. So instead of the trainee responding defensively to a statement like "the church doesn't care or God is not a loving God" (what is said), the trainee may respond to the emotion and experience behind such a statement made by a patient (what is meant). Responding to the emotion

---

9. Fitchett, *Assessing Spiritual Needs*, 48.
10. Krisak, "Facing the Faces of Grief," 39.

or experience behind an angry statement avoids responding to "content/head stuff." A response like "It sounds like you have had a really hurtful experience with the church" is much more likely to allow the patient to ventilate than if you were to defend the church and to say that the church is not like that at all.

Another model that I use in supervision with my trainees is what I have renamed the VDI Model (Ventilation—Differentiation—Integration). This model is a helpful reinforcement of Krisak's principle of "process not content is the key" but articulated in a slightly different way. The VDI model provides a helpful guide to trainees when faced with patients who ask them the "why" question. Many trainees would be tempted to respond to the "why" question from the "head" with intellectual answers and even quote scripture and give all sorts of good reasons why God does care even though the patient's experience and emotion may suggest otherwise.

Colin Johnstone[11] in his article suggests that the "why" question has two components which is best dealt with separately, the emotional component and the existential component. Johnstone recommends that the emotional component be dealt with first. Perhaps one of the most helpful sentences Johnstone makes in his article is this: "The person who sobs 'Why?' is not only asking a question, *but also making a statement about his or her feelings.*" This realization for me was hugely significant.

Once a trainee is able to see or to grasp this insight, he or she will have a better chance of not responding from the "head" or "existentially" but focus on the process or the emotional component thus enabling the patient to ventilate. This may also have the added advantage of the trainee no longer feeling such a great need to defend God or the church.

My supervisory stance and strategy here, would be to focus on the choices of interventions or responses that the trainee has made and also on when and why they were made and show them other alternative ways of hearing, understanding, and responding.

The drama triangle,[12] with its three roles of victim, persecutor, and rescuer, is a model that I have modified for supervision. Trainees easily grasp and understand the dangers of getting caught in such triangles and the effects it can have on their listening skills. Apart from the fact that such triangles are nearly always present in most pastoral situations, my rationale

---

11. Johnstone, "On Asking the Right Questions," 169–76.

12. Karpman, "Fairy Tales," 78–81, as cited in James and Jongeward, *Born to Win*, 92–97.

for the use of this model is to alert the trainees that once they are caught in such triangles, they unwittingly take sides emotionally and their listening is compromised.

My supervisory strategy is for trainees to learn to recognize what is happening and then to learn to step out of such a triangle. Trainees need to learn to avoid playing the rescuer or the persecutor, but to focus on listening to the feelings of the patient (victim) and to respond with empathy. This is being reflective rather than reactive.

Putting Theory into Practice

Teaching these models and new ways of listening and responding is one thing. Putting them into practice is quite another challenge. I remember an incident some years ago when I was teaching quite a large group and I made the point of pointing out the danger of having an agenda and when our need overshadowed the need of the patient.

I was attacked by a senior clergyman who felt that the gospel was so important that the need of the patient did not matter. I found myself in a classic drama triangle and felt under attack and was under attack. I could easily have attacked back and defended myself but decided to put into practice what I was trying to teach them by stepping out of the drama triangle and responded instead to this clergyman's disbelief and emotional anger at me.

I responded, "It sounds like you are very disappointed in what I am saying and you are struggling to understand why I won't share the gospel with every patient in hospital." I was pleasantly surprised that his assistant minister and the rest of the group took my side and supported me in this rather sensitive issue. Sadly, this clergyman was not open to exploring new ways of listening and responding and ministering to vulnerable patients.

BIBLIOGRAPHY

Cheston, Sharon E., and Robert J. Wicks, eds. *Essentials for Chaplains*. Mahwah, NJ: Paulist, 1993.
Clebsch, William A., and Charles R. Jaekle. *Pastoral Care in Historical Perspective*. Englewood Cliffs, NJ: Prentice Hall, 1964.
Clinebell, Howard. *Basic Types of Pastoral Care and Counseling*. Nashville: Abingdon, 1966.

Part II: Clinical Pastoral Education and Spiritual Practice

Fitchett, George. *Assessing Spiritual Needs: A Guide for Caregivers*. Minneapolis: Augsburg Fortress, 1993.
Hasty, Cathy. "Using a Modification of the Classic Drama Triangle to Enhance Pastoral Care." *Journal of Pastoral Care* 55 (2001) 147–57.
Hawkins, Peter, and Robin Shohet. *Supervision in the Helping Professions*. Milton Keynes, UK: Open University Press, 1989.
Hiltner, Seward. *Preface to Pastoral Theology*. Nashville: Abingdon, 1958.
James, Muriel, and Dorothy Jongeward. *Born to Win*. Philippines: Addison-Wesley, 1971.
Johnstone, Colin B. "On Asking the Right Question." *Journal of Pastoral Care* 35 (1981) 169–76.
Karpman, Stephen B. "Fairy Tales and Script Drama Analysis." *Transactional Analysis Bulletin* 26 (1968) 39–43.
Krisak, Anthony F. "Facing the Faces of Grief." In *Essentials for Chaplains*, edited by Sharon E. Cheston and and Robert J. Wicks, 34–47. Mahwah, NJ: Paulist, 1993.
Lartey, Emmanuel Y. *In Living Color: An Intercultural Approach to Pastoral Care and Counseling*. 2nd ed. London: Kingsley, 2003
Lester, Andrew D. *Hope in Pastoral Care and Counseling*. Louisville: Westminster John Knox, 1995.

7

A Fallen and Upside-Down World

Heather Robinson

INTRODUCTION

To help the elders in my local church learn and grow in their abilities to give pastoral care I presented them with a case study of a long suffering woman called Louise and introduced them to the action reflection model we use in our clinical pastoral education (CPE) program at the Mental Health CPE Centre. Using these two experiences—the actual visit to Louise and the group presentation—I describe how a loving community can approach the difficult problems in the world and give appropriate, sensitive pastoral and spiritual care to people in distress.

The psalmist cries out, "How long, O God? Will you forget me forever? How long will you hide your face from me?"[1] I hear the pain in these words. Whose life has not been touched by sorrow and suffering? Our world is filled with harrowing stories. On June 8, 2020, the World Health Organization stated it is estimated that up to one billion children aged two to seventeen years have experienced physical, sexual, or emotional violence

---

1. Ps 13.

or neglect in the past year.[2] Abuse of children is pervasive,[3] occurring within all countries, communities, races and religions, within institutions and within the home and family. The incidence is overwhelming and mind numbing. People do the wrong thing and inflict terrible suffering on others.

The United Nations, whose charter is to maintain international peace and security, condemns the widespread and systematic use of sexual violence as a tactic of war, terror, torture, and political repression, while struggling to deal with the sexual exploitation[4] and abuse of adults and children by some members of their own peacekeeping forces.[5] Sexual trafficking, sadistic sexual torture, raping of children and adults, whether opportunistic or systematic, by whomever, a peacekeeper, religious leader, parent or other family member, is a public health and social problem of immense proportions.

My faith tradition teaches about the love and peace of God. Jesus is known as the Prince of Peace who gave us the commandment to love God, and to love our neighbors as we love ourselves. He showed us how to do this. Two thousand years after his earthly ministry the level of suffering and incidence of abuse is scandalous. The nature of the world we live in is not what God wants for us. The world has fallen far from what it could be. It is upside down, confusing, chaotic, and messy. It is not always a safe place to be in. The church, while proclaiming the good news of God, has not always been a safe place and has betrayed, ignored, abandoned, and retraumatized some victims of abuse.

The prophet Micah says it is good to do justice, love kindness and walk humbly with our God.[6] How can we do this without becoming overwhelmed and exhausted? "How long must we cry out till justice rolls down like a river?" cries singer, songwriter, and theologian Robin Mann.[7] "How Long?" is a poignant song, whose chorus says, "Teach me to do what is

---

2. Hillis et al., "Global Prevalence," cited in WHO, "Violence Against Children."

3. WHO, *Global Status Report*.

4. In their study "Sexual Exploitation and Abuse in Peace Operations," Jasmine-Kim Westendorf and Louise Searle say that exploitation is "a useable although imperfect category" covering a range of sexual behavior, including sadistic sexual torture, child abuse, rape, sexual trafficking, and negotiated, consensual transactional sex. See https://academic.oup.com/ia/article-abstract/93/2/365/2982811, p. 375.

5. United Nations, "Sexual Violence in Conflict."

6. Micah 6:8.

7. Mann, "How Long?"

right: work in the darkness, trust in the light. And may love be the path I walk on."

These words are apt because they point to a pastoral response to injustice. Working in pastoral care at times means facing the dark consequences of injustice, as well as the darkness of despair, depression, the pain of loneliness, rejection, grief, and sadness. Working in pastoral care at times means facing the shocking, confronting realities of abuse. To do this well we need to learn and keep learning about what is most helpful and what is not helpful in such situations. The best teachers are the ones who receive care. And to care without love is not care at all.

CASE STUDY PART ONE: THE INCIDENT

I visited Louise while I was working as a spiritual care coordinator in a community aged care organization twenty years ago. Louise was in her late seventies and had numerous physical, emotional, and mental health difficulties. There was an air of desperation about her, like one who has sleepless nights and calls out to God to end their misery and take away their pain. She was a compelling figure because of her determination to live and overcome the struggles she was experiencing and which were increasing due to deteriorating health. She had already survived breast cancer, a mastectomy, open heart surgery and the removal of her gallbladder. She was proud of her successful rehabilitation from addiction to alcohol. A new challenge was failing eyesight due to the effects of glaucoma and increasing isolation due to frailty and disconnection from relatives.

On a follow up visit after accompanying Louise to an outpatient appointment at an eye clinic in a public hospital, I was momentarily stunned to hear her comment, "Wasn't that doctor awful! Did you see how close he came to me? It was like being *raped*." I remembered how the ophthalmologist had leaned forward to examine Louise's eyes, his knees touching, or almost touching, her knees. The mechanics of the tonometer he used to measure the pressure of fluid in Louise's eye restrained her head. The examination was awkward and uncomfortable for Louise and caused her anxiety to rise.

I do not remember my exact response to Louise's comment. At the time I felt inadequate and helpless. I was surprised and confronted to hear what she said. I acknowledged how awful it was for Louise. This validated her experience. I took her seriously and was a witness to her distress.

Part II: Clinical Pastoral Education and Spiritual Practice

GROUP DISCUSSION

After sharing part one of the case study with the group of elders I asked them to describe the impact on themselves of hearing this story. This was the second step in the five step theological reflection model developed by Rev. Alan Galt, outlined at the end of the chapter. The first step is giving a description of an incident or event which follows the well acclaimed method of beginning disciplined theological reflection with an experience.[8]

Attending to physical sensations, identifying the one or two central sensations felt most strongly, help us to capture the heart of the matter we are reflecting on.[9] We took time to listen to each other's responses to the questions "How did you feel hearing about Louise? What was the impact on yourself?" By taking time and not rushing to finish the five steps (we did not finish them), we heard more of the story and exercised our empathy. We practiced pastoral care by caring. We cared about what happened to Louise and we cared about what was happening to each other in the group. It was not an exercise to analyze the incident, but an experience of feeling and connecting. We were listening with our hearts.

A collective wisdom emerged as we listened and learned from each other. Responses included feeling probed, jolted, dismayed, alarmed, a gut-wrenching heart ache, heaviness, invaded, loss of control, overwhelmed, unsettled, and making connections to other instances of violation.

These responses were a way to connect more deeply with the story and broadened our understanding as different people had different reactions. This information and observations made was used to discern the spiritual needs of Louise. As we listened we were also able to care for ourselves and each other as the pain in the story touched the pain in our hearts.

I commend the openness of heart, loving compassion and inherent skills of listening attentively, as well as the honesty, thoughtful engagement and insights of the group who participated. Also they were aware of and accepted the limits of their knowledge and were keen to learn more.

After explaining the process of the theological reflection method we had started I shared with them my own reflection, *Case Study Part Two*, and in closing our session each group member shared how they were feeling. Responses included feeling inspired, encouraged, curious, free, stimulated, more confident, and exhausted.

---

8. The pastoral cycle in Thompson et al., *SCM Studyguide*, 50–60.
9. Killen and de Beer, *Art of Theological Reflection*, 88–89.

Realizing care can be effectively offered without knowing background details released one elder of the worry and concern about what was behind distressing and confronting statements a friend would sometimes make. They felt freed to listen more. Confidence increased with growing understanding of what is needed, and with recognizing what one is already doing well, and with what one can try to do in other situations. Being overwhelmed or exhausted can happen to any of us and reminds us of our limits.

CASE STUDY PART TWO: ULTIMATE CONCERNS, THEOLOGICAL TRUTHS, PASTORAL RESOURCES

I offer a reflection on what I see as Louise's ultimate concerns, or the issues which indicate her spiritual needs, some theological truths which apply to this situation and some thoughts on pastoral resources.

Louise needed a friend, someone on her side, a healthy relationship, someone to hear her, accept her without judging her or trying to change her, validating her worth (I am likeable, I have value), giving a sense of belonging, and easing the pain of loneliness. She died fifteen years ago, and I am still remembering her. Today, after all these years, I am a witness to Louise and her particular circumstances, and am more sensitive to the needs of people in distress. Through loving Louise my compassion grows.

I had a trusting relationship with Louise. I genuinely liked her. My aim was to be present with her, showing her respect, giving her attention and dignity, loving her and being a Christlike presence.

Describing the doctor's examination as rape suggests that Louise had experienced sexual violence in the past and that she was retraumatized by her experience in the eye clinic. Her personal space was violated. Though she walked in to the examination room of her own accord, in the moment of distress she was helpless. I think Louise was also traumatized by the many operations she had gone through, particularly open heart surgery.

The ophthalmologist had power as a male specialist, but was also in a system that expected him to attend to a lot of patients in an efficient (i.e., quick) way. He was unaware of the impact the examination was having on Louise, that it retraumatized her, or that a different approach may have given her a sense of control and safety and been less traumatic.

I do not know, or need to know, the details of the traumas that Louise experienced in her past. I am disturbed by Louise's story and other stories of trauma and abuse. I embrace feelings of disturbance that arise in me when I hear of the many instances of abuse in the world today—individual and systemic. Strangely, this gives me a sense of satisfaction, it is right to be outraged in the face of injustice.

Pastorally, it was effective to be alongside Louise as a calm, loving presence, and to be outraged and helpless together. Responding to her feelings was enough. In her book *The Cry: Understanding Church Abuse and Abusers*, Marlene Hickin outlines ways to support survivors of abuse, how to be "alongside a victim in a way that honours the second great commandment to love others as ourselves."[10] She also highlights ways well-intentioned Christians, while trying to be supportive and helpful, actually cause more harm through their lack of awareness, "imposing our own ideas and misconceptions," making presumptions and misunderstanding the situation.[11]

Focusing on abuse in the context of church communities, she examines when there is a disjunct between beliefs and behavior and the bewilderment and confusion that arises when a Christian leader teaches and preaches love, and is loving in some circumstances, but is discovered to have been abusive in other circumstances. Hickin mostly uses the word abuse as meaning "any manipulative usage of power."[12] The Christian community is not immune from these kinds of abuses. To be able to offer pastoral care in the world we need to recognize and face our own problems.

It is worthwhile to examine our beliefs, understanding, and values, particularly in relation to God's love. What does it mean to be loved by God? What does it mean to love God and to love our neighbors as ourselves? These are some of the questions we look at in depth in our CPE programs.

Caring for Louise and others challenged me to examine my beliefs and face the disturbing realities of a fallen world. In my relationship with Louise and others I heard (and keep hearing) a call to support and advocate for the Blue Knot Foundation (https://www.blueknot.org.au/). This Australian national charity empowers recovery from complex trauma, providing support, education, and resources for adult survivors of complex trauma and their families and communities. They have developed *Trauma Informed Care and Practice Guidelines* which have been acclaimed worldwide and which are available on their website. One of their publications, *Talking*

---

10. Hickin, *The Cry*, 156.
11. Hickin, *The Cry*, 161.
12. Hickin, *The Cry*, 12.

About Trauma, is a valuable resource for pastoral carers.[13] In plain English they explain why the trauma-informed principles of safety, trustworthiness, choice, collaboration, and empowerment are important and how to apply them.[14]

Their website states, "We should not underestimate the capacity of positive interactions, even in routine interactions, to be soothing and validating. . . . Positive experiences of relationships are central to trauma recovery. They are also important to general well-being. By employing trauma-informed principles, we can build a 'trauma-informed' society. This creates possibilities for psychological and physical healing on a grand scale."[15]

I would add to this statement, *this creates possibilities for spiritual healing*. Professor, writer, and theologian Henri Nouwen knew about the benefit of being with another person as a friend or companion, being present with them for their sake:

> When we honestly ask ourselves which persons in our lives mean the most to us, we often find that it is those who instead of giving much advice, solutions or cures, have chosen rather to share our pain and touch our wounds with a gentle and tender hand. The friend who can be silent with us in a moment of despair or confusion, who can stay with us in an hour of grief and bereavement, who can tolerate not-knowing, not-curing, not-healing and face with us the reality of our powerlessness that is the friend who cares.[16]

Being present with another in the way Nouwen describes is comforting, makes a difference, and is the best pastoral resource we can use. As my colleague Rosemarie Say from the Mental Health CPE Centre often says, "Don't just do something. Stand there."[17] I believe God is there with us in the standing. And I believe and have hope in the transforming power of God. When God is with us, all will be well, and God is with us in the waiting for all to be well. Another important belief for me is that love does

---

13. Kezelman and Stavropoulos, *Talking about Trauma*.

14. Kezelman and Stavropoulos, in *Talking about Trauma*, reference the five trauma informed principles of Fallot and Harris, *Creating Cultures of Trauma-Informed Care*.

15. See the Blue Knot Foundation website, https://www.blueknot.org.au/Resources/Information/Trauma-Informed-Care-and-Practice.

16. Nouwen, *Out of Solitude*, 38.

17. A saying attributed to theatrical producer Martin Gabel at the first rehearsal of Irwin Shaw's play *The Assassin*, https://quoteinvestigator.com/2014/03/22/stand-there/.

no harm. I am moved by Isa 43:2, which says, "A bruised reed he will not break, and a dimly burning wick he will not quench; he will faithfully bring forth justice."

Yet sometimes I have to look closely to see that the reed is not broken, the wick not quenched. If I only look at the suffering and the injustice I am blinded and cannot see what God is doing. When discussing this case with experienced pastoral carer and elder Pamela Briggs she saw that Louise was brave and able to take risks. I saw the spirit of life in Louise, her sense of fun and her passion for justice.

I cannot answer the questions, *Why do people hurt other people?* and *Why do people suffer?* but I do not give up and I use the energy of anger to speak out against injustice and support and advocate for the Blue Knot Foundation. In doing this I become a witness to the power of God to shine light among the pain, chaos, muck, and mess of life and bring love, comfort, and hope to the weary and down hearted. When my heart is open to give and receive love I see God at work in the world, and I see the beauty of the person before me. Whenever I have my eyes checked I start a conversation with the optometrist about the Blue Knot Foundation. This action is a legacy to Louise.

PERSONAL IMPACT

I cannot answer difficult questions about suffering, but I do have a response. The Psalm quoted at the beginning of this essay was used in a liturgy for a prayer vigil held weekly at South Sydney Uniting Church during the lockdown due to the COVID-19 pandemic, and wove the Psalm 13 with Matt 10:40–42, the Gospel for the day.[18]

> Prayer
>
> *How long, O God? Will you forget me forever?*
> *How long will you hide your face from me?*
>
> SILENCE
>
> *How long, O God? Will you forget me forever?*
> *How long will you hide your face from me?*
>
> SILENCE
>
> *How long must I wrestle with my anguish,*

---

18. Prayer Vigil, Ordinary Sunday 13, Year A, South Sydney Uniting Church, June 28, 2020.

and wallow in despair all day long?
How long will my enemy win over me?
RESPONSE: I am here. Welcome me.

I trust in your love;
my heart rejoices in the deliverance you bring.
I'll sing to you, God,
for being so good to me.
RESPONSE: I am here. Welcome me.
I am in the holy one. I am in the prophet.
I am in the disciple. I am in the lowly one.
I am in the one before you.

With my colleagues in clinical pastoral education, the students whom I supervise, the congregation with whom I worship and pray, and the people who are before me, I learn and grow in serving God. It has the cost of opening my heart and facing and embracing painful and uncomfortable realities. It means feeling the sadness and grieving the pain and suffering before me and in me. But how would it be if we were to go through life and not notice, not wake up to the suffering around us? How would it be not to pause, listen, and care? How would it be if we were not to shed a tear? And at the same time, how would it be if we were to go through life and not be grateful? How would it be if we did not notice the beauty around and within? How would it be if we did not welcome the one before us?

One of the lines from the Orthodox funeral service says "Weeping at the grave creates the song Alleluia." I have found this to be true. In welcoming the one before me, I receive the gift of love and compassion and my heart fills with gratitude, while I also have a place in my heart that weeps for the pain and suffering in the world.

CONCLUSION

There is no excuse for abuse. It is wrong and as a society we must hold to account people who have abused others. It takes a purposeful commitment to listen to victims of abuse and be supportive to them. It requires a willingness to learn and keep learning about what is helpful to those in need and to examine our own assumptions, values, and beliefs. Every person has a quality of uniqueness, so each pastoral relationship and each interaction requires reflection and discernment in order that we give appropriate, sensitive pastoral and spiritual care. Although it can be confronting and disturbing, uncomfortable and challenging, it is also very rewarding and is what is required of us when we love God, love our neighbors and love ourselves.

SUPPLEMENTARY: THEOLOGICAL REFLECTION TEMPLATE

The theological reflection template developed by Rev. Alan Galt is used by students in our CPE programs to reflect on their pastoral encounters. During group supervision the written reflections are shared and this has proved to be a valuable learning experience.

1. The incident, event or specific interaction (arising in your pastoral interaction).
2. Its impact on me (how I felt in that situation).
3. Ultimate concerns present (significant issues beyond which nothing is more important).
4. Theological reflection (what theological truths apply in this situation? What message from my faith, or from the faith of the resident, are relevant?) *or* Theological reflection: where is God in this situation?
5. Pastoral resources needed here (e.g., pastoral presence, pastoral conversation, prayer, stories and examples from the scriptures and sacred teachings, religious ritual, liturgy, sacrament, discussion of spiritual themes).

BIBLIOGRAPHY

Blue Knot Foundation. *Trauma-Informed Care and Practice*. 2020. https://www.blueknot.org.au/Resources/Information/Trauma-Informed-Care-and-Practice.

Fallot, Roger D., and Maxine Harris. *Creating Cultures of Trauma-Informed Care (CCTIC): A Self-Assessment and Planning Protocol*. Washington, DC: Community Connections, 2009. https://www.theannainstitute.org/CCTICSELFASSPP.pdf.

Hickin, Marlene. *The Cry: Understanding Church Abuse & Abusers*. 2nd ed. Hornsby, Australia: Kimbrada, 2013.

Hillis Susan, et al. "Global Prevalence of Past-Year Violence against Children: A Systematic Review and Minimum Estimates." *Pediatrics* 137 (2016) e20154079.

Kezelman, Cathy, and Pam Stavropoulos. *Talking about Trauma: Guide to Everyday Conversations for the General Public*. Blue Knot Foundation, 2017. https://www.blueknot.org.au/Survivors-Supporters/supporting-survivors/talking-about-trauma.

Killen, Patricia O'Connell, and John de Beer. *The Art of Theological Reflection*. New York: Crossroad, 1994.
Mann, Robin. "How Long?" 2001. http://www.robinmann.com.au/My-songs-All-Together-for-Good-How-Long-pg30929.html.
Nouwen, Henri. *Out of Solitude: Three Meditations on the Christian Life*. Notre Dame: Ave Maria, 2004.
Thompson, Judith, et al. *SCM Studyguide to Theological Reflection*. London: SCM, 2008.
United Nations. *Sexual Violence in Conflict: Youth Speak Out through the Arts*. 2020. https://www.un.org/en/exhibits/page/sexual-violence-conflict.
Westendorf, Jasmine-Kim, and Louise Searle. "Sexual Exploitation and Abuse in Peace Operations: Trends, Policy Responses, and Future Directions." *International Affairs* 93 (2017) 365–87. https://academic.oup.com/ia/article/93/2/365/2982811.
World Health Organization. *Global Status Report on Violence Prevention 2014*. Geneva: WHO, 2014. https://www.who.int/violence_injury_prevention/violence/status_report/2014/en/
———. "Violence Against Children." WHO, June 8, 2020. https://www.who.int/news-room/fact-sheets/detail/violence-against-children.

8

"CPE Has Changed My Life!"—A Constant Student Refrain

ROSEMARIE SAY

INTRODUCTION[1]

"CLINICAL PASTORAL EDUCATION IS an area of education in which I am passionate. . . . What an awakening and rewarding experience I had. It changed my life," enthused Her Excellency Mrs. Linda Hurley, addressing the twenty-fifth annual ANZACPE Conference in 2015.[2] For twenty years, I have heard this recurring theme of transformation in feedback from students, young and old, and from all walks of life—professions, cultures, and faith traditions. Using snippets of their observations, along with anecdotes and references, I will explore what it is about the CPE experience in a psychiatric hospital that has this effect.

---

1. Excepting for students, pseudonyms will be used.
2. Linda Hurley is the wife of His Excellency General the Honourable David John Hurley AC DSC (retd.), who was sworn in as the twenty-seventh governor-general of the Commonwealth of Australia, July 1, 2019.

WHAT IS LIFE CHANGING ABOUT CPE?

According to Mike (2020), "CPE turned my life around. CPE is not about the experience—it's about *reflecting* on the experience. And that's the essence, the uniqueness of CPE. It's a structure that becomes part of your life."

SO WHAT IS CPE?

Clinical pastoral education (CPE) is an "action-reflection" process, providing opportunities for supervised, intense pastoral encounters in a variety of circumstances where students pursue their individual *Learning Goals* in *Personal Growth; Professional Competence; Pastoral Identity*. Self-awareness is paramount. Through constant feedback from peers, mentors, clients, and supervisors, students develop new understanding of their own humanity and the needs of those to whom they offer pastoral care.

In order to complete their four hundred hours of training, students meet and visit at the hospital one day a week for six months. This enables adequate time for assignments and, in particular, the valuable reflection needed between program sessions.

MY FIRST LESSON: WE ARE HUMAN BEINGS, NOT HUMAN DOINGS!

I still remember "Mrs. Smith" from twenty years ago. Early in my CPE training I sat for twenty minutes with her. Elderly and depressed, she did not respond to any of my attempts to engage. She just sat in silence, looking at the floor. I felt helpless and useless. I was relieved when a nurse came to take her elsewhere. She then rose slowly to her feet—and turned imploringly to me: "Will you be here when I get back?"

With eight monosyllabic words, Mrs. Smith taught me that I could bring comfort, light, and hope by just sitting and staying with people in the darkness and utter aloneness of their suffering and despair. That is what Jesus needed in Gethsemane when he found the disciples sleeping. And he said to Peter, "So, could you not watch with me one hour?" (Matt 26:40 NIV).

That first simple experience of staying with the helplessness, discomfort, and humiliation of "not knowing" and "not fixing" was a powerful kick start to my transition from nurse to chaplain—to "be" rather than to "do." A significant aspect of suffering is the alone-ness, and we can take that away just by being there. The "ministry of presence" is now the bedrock of my practice.

Our Mental Health CPE (MHCPE) training is based on the model espoused by an American, Anton Theophilus Boisen (1876–1965). Determined to make sense of his own psychotic episodes and psychiatric hospital admissions, he emerged as a "wounded healer."[3] In the 1920s, he worked as a chaplain, challenging tradition by taking theological students into these institutions for their edification—just to listen to the stories and make connections. "I have sought not to begin with the ready-made formulations contained in books but with the living human documents and with actual social conditions in all their complexity."[4]

"HERE BE DRAGONS . . ."

I have always been drawn to the marginalized. Decades ago, the psychiatric hospital where I trained as a nurse was known as "The Looney Bin"—a dumping ground for people who were shunned by society for being different and not fitting in to the expected norm. But why? After all, who is "normal"? As Andrew Denton says, "We all walk the tight-rope of normality." And any one of us at any time can fall off.

I was shocked and horrified by the inhumane conditions, the physical cruelty, and the barbaric "shock treatment" (electroconvulsive therapy), which was given without anaesthetic or muscle relaxant, and often threatened as punishment. This was what drove me to return to a psychiatric hospital—to lay the ghosts that gave me nightmares for years. Moving from nursing to chaplaincy, I found that conditions have changed—but still the stigma remains.

Stigma results in rejection, and compounds the isolation and suffering of mental health issues. It is a barrier to relationship. As Friedrich Nietzsche, a nineteenth-century philosopher who suffered a psychiatric illness, reputedly lamented, "And those who were seen dancing were thought to be insane by those who could not hear the music."[5] My ultimate aim, as a

---

3. Nouwen, *Wounded Healer*.

4. Boisen, *Exploration*, 185.

5. Friedrich Nietzsche (1844–1900) was a German philosopher who suffered a psychiatric illness. This quote has generally been attributed to him but with no other details.

MHCPE Educator, is to dispel the stigma and to engage and attune students to "hear the music" and appreciate the "dancing."

GO THERE; STAY THERE; LISTEN!

At first, however, working with a largely long-term treatment-resistant mentally-ill population is strange and confronting. Boisen warns of the hazards in going out into the "raw material of life,"[6] "with its delicate and baffling inner conflicts."[7] It is normal for students to feel anxious in this new situation.

They are venturing beyond the walls of the church to tread dark unfamiliar corridors. They are entering the nightmare world of intractable suffering and suicide. They might see themselves mirrored in the eyes of the depressed, deranged, and demented. They sit helplessly in the unedited scrap heap of humanity. It is too easy to slip over the edge when life's path becomes narrow and rocky.

"How do we respond?" they ask, when confronted with delusional material. It is difficult as the beliefs are fixed, but the content, often very disturbing, is not real. However, what the person is feeling *is* real, and that is what we can affirm and work with pastorally. It is not the job of the pastoral carer to reality-test—that is work for other professionals. Our job is to *listen*. And to take them seriously. Hugh Mackay maintains that the desire to be taken seriously is the most important human need.[8] It is encapsulated in the plea: "Please recognise and acknowledge me as a unique individual."[9]

BEING COMFORTABLE WITH THE UNCOMFORTABLE

It is so much easier to avoid these people. However, as students reflect, they realize that *everyone* is trying to avoid them. Shirley described her ministry as "just to love them in all circumstances." It works. "There is no fear in love. But perfect love drives out fear" (1 John 4:18).

It takes resolve to enter the raw, dark places where people are so tormented, but that is where we are called—to be the face of their God—even

---

6. Boisen, *Exploration*, 250.
7. Boisen, *Exploration*, 263.
8. Mackay, *What Makes Us Tick?*
9. Mackay, *What Makes Us Tick?*, 2.

to "walk through the valley of the shadow of death" (Ps 23:4) with them. "They're not comfortable places, but they're life-changing," pondered George. As students struggle with the stories, the unpredictability and unfairness of life, they marvel at the resilience of the human spirit. They are being ministered to by the outcasts of society. They have had to look deep within themselves for the courage to continue . . . and have found it sitting opposite them—in this very institution.

Laurence wrote, "The scales fell from my eyes regarding this great privilege of ministry to the churchless—the least, the lost, the lonely. My first year of CPE in 2016 was life-changing."

Generally, at the end of a CPE program, students acknowledge their awareness of "seeing differently."

> Earth's crammed with heaven,
> And every common bush afire with God;
> But only he who sees, takes off his shoes,
> The rest sit round it and pluck blackberries.[10]

SAFETY, TRUST, AND RISK IN CPE TRAINING

First "Know Thyself." This adage was reputedly inscribed in the forecourt of the Temple of Apollo at Delphi, and subsequently became a touchstone for western philosophers. In order to know others we need to know ourselves.

My mantra is, "Be where *they* are at, but be firmly grounded in who *you* are, and where you are coming from"—emotionally, psychologically, and theologically.

Each CPE day opens with, "Where are you, and how are you feeling at this moment?" For some students, this mindfulness practice is a revelation and becomes a daily discipline—often the beginning of a process of discovery of their authentic selves . . .

And then BE yourself! The act of being "genuine" or "authentic" encourages others to be real, fostering honest relationships through shared trust and vulnerability. This helps the students to bond, and they consistently describe the CPE group interactions as nourishing—and an "oasis" in their energy-depleting week.

Hopefully and usually, students model their pastoral approach on their group experience of genuineness, along with empathy and unconditional

---

10. Browning, "From 'Aurora Leigh,'" 152.

positive regard—the other components of Carl Rogers' "Therapeutic Triad" endorsed by Clinebell.[11]

As supervisors, we walk with students, picking them up when they fall down. Winnicott's concept of being held and supported[12] offers them a safe space to process, and learn from, the emotions aroused by unsettling pastoral interactions. We gently challenge them when they say, "I can't do this." We know they *can*. We have been there!

As a student, I was advised, "When you come to a door you don't want to go through, that's probably where you are most needed." And it was those doors that daunted most that were the ones that provided the most learning and growth through supervision and counseling. So there comes a time when students might need a gentle nudge to take the risk. It is scary at the edge. Even when their wings are ready, many a fledgling student needs encouragement before they will venture from the familiarity of the nest. And then they fly. Transformation is happening. It is the beginning of a new adventure!

FORGET THE LABEL AND THE "US AND THEM" MENTALITY

Initially, students ask, "What's *wrong* with that patient?" It is normal—we are hard-wired to fix. But that is what every other professional in the hospital does. As an ex-nurse, I had to overcome my medical curiosity and disregard the diagnosis. So I challenge students to "look at what's *right* with that person," and to affirm that by honouring their inherent goodness and uniqueness. And they do.

Laurence demonstrated his appreciation in a 2017 report:

> Our thought for today was "Normality is a paved road: it's comfortable to walk, but no flowers grow on it" (Vincent Van Gogh). Since I read this, I thought all morning about how truly blessed I am to walk a path with flowers—here at the hospital and at work.[13]

---

11. Clinebell and McKeever, *Basic Types of Pastoral Care*, 465–66.

12. Cited in Hawkins and Shohet, *Supervision*, 3.

13. Vincent Willem Van Gogh (1853–1897) was a Dutch post-impressionist painter who suicided after years of psychotic episodes and psychiatric hospital admissions.

Part II: Clinical Pastoral Education and Spiritual Practice

EVERYONE BECOMES A TEACHER AND A LEARNER[14]

It takes a humble shift for students to see the patient as the one who will be their teacher for this year. In turn, we supervisors benefit from the students' fresh insights. The message that "the least is the greatest" peppers the Gospels and offends conventional thinking. It is a back-to-front, upside-down message echoed in words such as "The last will be first and the first will be last" (Matt 20:16), and "Unless you change and become like little children, you will never enter the kingdom of heaven" (Matt 18:3).

Willard Wagner warns of the danger of academic seduction in his account of a young student-nurse who connected so well with a patient that she went off to do library research on his diagnosis and medication.[15] When she came back armed with her knowledge and answers, she found she had lost the relationship—the connection of "beginner's mind" was no longer there. As in 1 Cor 8:1, "Knowledge puffs up, but love builds up."

Richard Rohr explains:

> This is precisely how transformation differs from simply acquiring facts and information. Whereas information will often inflate the ego, transformation utterly humbles us. In that moment, we know how much *we have not known up to now, and still surely do not know!* Such humility is a good and probably necessary starting place and, I would say, the very seat of Wisdom.[16]

Deacon George came into the CPE program, not knowing what to do or say. I shared from my own experience: "It's OK to feel helpless." Subsequently, he brought a report on his interaction with a suffering elderly man. He wrote, "I realized there was nothing I could fix. I realized there was nothing I could say. So I sat mainly in silence . . ." It worked. He concluded, "Despite all the theological lectures I have attended over the past three years, I received my greatest lesson in theology from a gentle ninety-year-old man who had never studied theology in his life."

CPE TEACHING APPROACH

A hazard of the academic profession—or of book learning in general—can be intellectual arrogance and remoteness, and this can flow on to the

---

14. Mezirow, *Transformative Learning in Practice*, 80.
15. Wagner, "Voices on Psychiatry," 156.
16. Rohr, "Wisdom Is Loving."

students. Parker Palmer stresses the importance of identity, integrity, and connectedness. "Good teachers join self and subject and students in the fabric of life," but "bad teachers," whose "words float somewhere in front of their faces, like the balloon speech in cartoons," distance themselves from subject and student.[17]

While pedagogy keeps students feeling secure, they can become disconnected from humanity: "We don't want to do anything relational because we are tired," is a common attitude. There are too many tired teachers and a lot of tired learners. Where is the relationship, the wonder, the curiosity?[18]

SHALL WE DANCE?

It can be daunting relating to someone who is different. If we approach lightly with no expectations, it is liberating. Winnicott describes "learning as being most creative when it emerges in play."[19] Dorothy wrote of her effortless connection with a thought-disordered woman: "I didn't try to understand her. I just went on a magical journey with her—and we played like children joyfully together, somewhere in the ether." As Einstein postulated, "Imagination is more important than knowledge. Knowledge is limited. Imagination encircles the world."

In a conference presentation *Shall We Dance?* I hypothesized that we can "dance in the gap"—the gap where society fractures, but souls can touch.[20] If we come, not as professionals with all the answers, but on an equal footing, our patients will teach us the steps. I cautioned that here we are entering a different world. Working from a stable base is vital. This is where intensive CPE supervision is essential to stay oriented and not "get lost on the dance-floor."

In a verbatim excerpt, Karen accompanies "Harriet" as a fellow human being:

> *Harriet: "I pray for orphan children, tequila on the water and washing dishes in the ocean."*
>
> *Karen simply repeats the prayer and they smile together.*

17. Palmer, *Courage to Teach*, 11.
18. Dutney, "Remembering the Future," from my SCD Learning and Teaching Theology Conference notes.
19. Cited in Hawkins and Shohet, *Supervision*, 7.
20. Say, "Shall We Dance."

> Harriet: "I have seen the stars in many colors from the drugs."
> Karen responds, "Sounds beautiful..."
> They sit happily together in silence...

Throughout the whole interaction, Karen continued to "dance," keeping perfect step with Harriet, and valuing, not judging, her uniqueness. Karen had come alive in her ministry. Clinebell advocates adding personal aliveness to our repertoire of approaches: "Aliveness is contagious! So is deadness!"[21]

Max (2016) admitted:

> When I first met "Roger," I didn't know what he was talking about—it was total fantasy—crazy stuff! I had no idea what was going on in his head. Then one day he said out of the blue, "You don't listen to me, do you?" I was very surprised—and ashamed. From that moment on, I decided to try to enter his world and listen in CPE mod—attentively and deeply. And when I did, it was a most fantastic exhilarating journey. I began to really enjoy my time with him!

LEARNING FROM, AND INSPIRED BY, THE "LIVING HUMAN DOCUMENT"

> ...which is my work, which is mostly standing still
> and learning to be astonished...
>
> —Mary Oliver

"Fred" had been institutionalized most of his life. His only possession was a brown paper bag full of broken windscreen glass. He called them his "diamonds." At his funeral, we heard a recording of Fred singing his song, "The Magic of Life." It is chastening to meet people who express gratitude for the little things that we take for granted.

A constantly recurring theme in our students' feedback is that they feel "grounded" on their ward visits. They are reminded of how we tend to fret over superficial concerns and can easily become consumed by our societal drive to succeed and achieve. John, weighed down with his problems, came

---

21. Clinebell and McKeever, *Basic Types of Pastoral Care*, 467–68.

back from a visit to a double-locked ward. He reported feeling humbled and uplifted when greeted by a long-term patient with, "It's a beautiful day. The sun is shining."

People "on the edge" are resilient survivors who have overcome years of adversity, and now bear their day-to-day challenges, with the "fruit of the Spirit" (Gal 5:22–23). They understand and care for each other with compassion, generosity, and patience that puts me to shame. They have no masks, pretences or defences. They have nothing, but would give you anything. Their props and possessions have been stripped away. As one patient said, "This is how we stand before God—no layers." And without these layers, they are surely closer to God than we are.

Josephine (2015) reflected:

> I found CPE to be both challenging and transformative. I learned so much from the formal teaching, the group process and most especially from the patients. They showed me the strength and courage required to love from the depths of powerlessness. And they shone with the beauty and power of that, clear to those who take the time to notice, as the program teaches us to do.

I invited a highly qualified professional to join me for a CPE students' pastoral group. This was conducted with six patients in a long-term psychiatric ward. He came with muted enthusiasm as he felt he'd "been there, done that" plenty of times—what could he learn? Afterward he wrote an animated account of his visit, affirming the value of being willing to enter their world and learn from them:

> What I saw today blew me away. Firstly I was able to see them not as patients but people. . . . As a doctor and a priest, I would be considered "wise and prudent," and today's encounter reminded me about how the downcast, the "low functioning" have received a great revelation of God that I may not have beheld as well as I ought. . . . Even though I attended offering my time to these people, I was receiving so much more in return.

TRANSFORMATION IN THE LIMINAL SPACE

Kelly writes about "attentive waiting" in the liminal space of transition.[22] When we are with people in crisis or in any meaningful way, we often slip

---

22. Kelly, *Personhood and Presence*, 24–48.

into this space of just *being*—"hard but holy moments"[23] of not knowing, and being totally open to what is present.

How many times have I heard the words: "I felt privileged to be there"? As with Moses and his burning bush encounter (Exod 3:5), we can transcend the mundane, in a suspended moment of time, for a glimpse of the infinite. "There is an up-side for being around these people who struggle, for as we draw nearer to them we find God. I find the most divine and transformative encounters with them" (Mel, 2018). In emptying ourselves ("kenosis") to be a conduit for God's grace and love, we are transfused with a surge of compassionate energy. This phenomenon, described by Harrison as "exquisite empathy,"[24] revitalizes rather than drains, and fuels my passion for this ministry.

As author and athlete, Jean-Paul Bedard wrote, "In hospitals, how thin the veil is that separates the physical from the holy. The veil separating the mundane and the transcendent had been pushed aside for the briefest of moments. And I will be forever changed by that glimpse of the divine."[25]

THEOLOGICAL/SPIRITUAL REFLECTION—A VITAL COMPONENT OF CPE

We are created as unique spiritual beings, and as Dutney expressed, "God is up to something in every situation and in every person's life."[26] It is exciting and liberating to have an open mind; to recognize God's working in each person; to participate, and embrace the challenges!

In 2005, I assisted Rev. Alan Galt in conducting the first multi-faith Introductory CPE at Prince of Wales Hospital, Randwick. It was an edifying experience, spiced with the life journeys of people from all faith traditions. Catholic Michael was astonished: "I've never been in such a large and diverse group where everyone was focused on learning how to serve others."

In dialoguing we respected the need to "Walk humbly with your God" (Mic 6:8). The reward was to find theological barriers crumble as we concentrated on our common theme of serving with love and compassion for humanity. Students, maintaining their integrity, honoured their traditions by sharing resources and passages, enriching the group with new insights.

23. Kelly, *Personhood and Presence*, 26.
24. Harrison and Westwood, "Preventing Vicarious Traumatization," 213.
25. Bedard, "Touching the Veil."
26. Dutney, "Remembering," 16.

As one student summarized, "We are all children of God trying to find our way home the best way we can."

Rather than having our theology diluted, we explored, clarified, and strengthened our beliefs as we strove to articulate them while acknowledging others. This is an important part of CPE. "Unless pastors are able to tap into their own source of being, to find their own voice, to sing their own song, regardless of the key, they remain robots dancing to another's tune."[27]

CONCLUSION

Students are attracted to Mental Health CPE from all walks of life to be "companions on the Journey" as they wander, ponder, and wonder through the corridors of a unique library of Boisen's "living human documents." Here, they come face to face with not only those living in the shadows, but also the shadows of their own true selves. Having the spirit to meet this challenge, and to reflect on the experience, is the resolve that transforms.

Shaped by their individual *learning goals*, every student has a different journey. However, the common thread (in MHCPE) is letting go of the stigma, and growing in understanding and love of those whom others fear and reject. "Go back to the Milky Way where you come from," shouted "Bert" angrily to Ros. "You don't belong here." "It's OK . . . you have a good day." Ros was unfazed. The next day "Bert" welcomed her with a flower.

Gradually, as they begin to view life through a more tolerant lens, students develop a multitude of people skills, especially the ability to stay calm and defuse a crisis. Learning how to *really* listen improves the quality of their relationships in every situation and in every aspect of their lives.

CPE offers a theological challenge with the potential for many an epiphany. Students often start the program keen to take *their* God to the wards. When they get there they find a bigger God waiting in the darkest and most desolate places. This is holy ground on which, entering, we take off our shoes and stand in awe of each other.

And it brings to life my favorite verses of Scripture: Jesus said, "I was sick and you looked after me, I was in prison and you came to visit me." . . . "Whatever you did for one of the least of these brothers and sisters of mine, you did for me" (Matt 25:36, 40).

---

27. Gilbert, *Pastoral Care*, 99.

Part II: Clinical Pastoral Education and Spiritual Practice

BIBLIOGRAPHY

Bedard, Jean-Paul. "Touching the Veil of Thin Places." *HuffPost Life*, March 12, 2014. https://www.huffpost.com/entry/touching-the-veil-of-thin_b_6256592.

Boisen, Anton T. *The Exploration of the Inner World: A Study of Mental Disorder and Religious Experience*. Chicago: Willett, Clark, 1936.

Browning, Elizabeth B. "From 'Aurora Leigh.'" In *The Oxford Book of English Mystical Verse*, edited by Daniel H. S. Nicholson and Arthur H. E. Lee, 150–52. Oxford: Clarendon, 1917.

Clinebell, Howard, and Bridget Clare McKeever. *Basic Types of Pastoral Care and Counseling: Resources for the Ministry of Healing and Health*. 3rd ed. Nashville: Abingdon, 2011.

Dutney, Andrew. "Remembering the Future: The Contribution of Historical Research to Innovation in Theological Education." In *Wondering about God Together: Research-led Learning and Teaching in Theological Education*, edited by Les Ball and Peter Bolt, 1–18. Macquarie Park, Australia: SCD Press, 2018.

Gilbert, Binford W. *Pastoral Care of Depression: A Guidebook*. New York: Routledge, 1998.

Harrison, Richard L., and Marvin J. Westwood. "Preventing Vicarious Traumatization of Mental Health Therapists: Identifying Protective Practices." *Psychotherapy: Theory, Research, Practice, Training* 46 (2009) 203–19. Washington, DC: American Psychological Association. https://www.mindfulheartprograms.net/uploads/1/1/6/3/116300257/4._harrison___westwood_2009_preventing_vt.pdf.

Hawkins, Peter, and Robin Shohet. *Supervision in the Helping Professions*. 3rd ed. Maidenhead, UK: Open University Press, 2006.

Hurley, Linda. Opening ceremony address, 25th anniversary of the Australia and New Zealand Association of Clinical Pastoral Education, Mary Mackillop Memorial Chapel, Sydney, September 13, 2015.

Kelly, Ewan. *Personhood and Presence: Self as a Resource for Spiritual and Pastoral Care*. London: T. & T. Clark International, 2012.

Mackay, Hugh. *What Makes Us Tick? The Ten Desires That Drive Us*. Sydney: Hachette Australia, 2010.

Mezirow, Jack. *Transformative Learning in Practice*. San Francisco: Jossey-Bass, 2009.

Nouwen, Henri J. M. *The Wounded Healer: Ministry in Contemporary Society*. New York: Doubleday Image, 1972.

Oliver, Mary. "The Messenger." In *Thirst: Poems by Mary Oliver*. Boston: Beacon, 2006.

Palmer, Parker J. *The Courage to Teach—Exploring the Inner Landscape of a Teacher's Life*. San Francisco: Jossey-Bass, 1997.

Rohr, Richard. "Wisdom Is Loving." Center for Action and Contemplation. February 21, 2020. https://cac.org/wisdom-is-loving-2020-02-21/#gsc.tab=0.

Say, Rosemarie. "Shall We Dance?" Mental Health Ministry Paper, presented at the Uniting*Care* NSW.ACT Pastoral Care Conference ("Dancing in the Gap"), St Joseph's Retreat Centre, Baulkham Hills, NSW, October 8–11, 2013.

Wagner, Willard. "The Voices on Psychiatry: Inner Tumult and the Quest for Meaning." In *Hospital Ministry: The Role of the Chaplain Today*, edited by Lawrence E. Holst, 151–62. New York: Crossroads, 1990.

PART III

ANTON THEOPHILUS BOISEN AND CLINICAL PASTORAL EDUCATION FROM AN APOCALYPTIC ASPECT

9

Apocalyptic Thinking, the Incarnational Jesus, and Clinical Pastoral Education in the Secular World

A Critical Perspective

Sang Taek Lee

INTRODUCTION

FOR MY DOCTORAL DISSERTATION at the University of Sydney, I researched millennial hope from a social perspective. Since studying clinical pastoral education (CPE), I have thought how apocalyptic thinking can apply to CPE. While researching the books of Anton Boisen, I was moved by his mental suffering and his struggles, impressed by his creative concept of the *living human document*, and his deep pastoral and theological insights that communicate a modern sense beyond the theological understanding of his day. It is within all these elements that I discovered an apocalyptic insight to his theological understanding.

What do CPE, apocalyptic thinking and the incarnation of Jesus in a secular society have in common with Boisen? Apocalyptic thinking is often linked to social crisis, while the role of CPE is to care for those overwhelmed by mental, physical, and spiritual crises in the world. How do we understand CPE through the lens of apocalyptic thinking? The Christian belief arising from Jesus' incarnation should aim to reflect Christian practice with the questions that arise in everyday life.

However, thinking in apocalyptic terms does not necessarily lead one to become an apocalyptist. Rather, apocalyptic thinking can be thought of as a way of bringing new hope to society in the context of oppression or despair. Apocalyptic thinking leads us to understand clearly that the incarnation of Jesus is what he has done for the world.

In this essay, I do not use the term *apocalyptic thinking* to mean a particular thought, ideology or a stream of theology with a defined systematic structure. Apocalyptic thinking is an open expression of the daily experiences of one's life. The early church expressed this through their beliefs in an apocalyptic setting where they faced suffering, oppression, and persecution, and waiting for the messiah to free them from this hardship in their historical, social, political, and spiritual context. It is not an academic thought, but a reflection of their daily life relating to the coming Jesus. Therefore, apocalyptic thinking represents the values of the early church and Christian tradition by expressing the meaning of their belief and commitment to Christ.

Clinical pastoral education is a practice which seeks to offer acknowledgment and support to vulnerable people who are facing significant personal crises (for example, physical or mental health) or who may have been excluded or marginalized from society. They are welcomed, accepted, and cared for by God's love and compassion, which is revealed through the suffering and resurrection of Jesus Christ in the world. Boisen shows us the ability to link personal experience, social concerns, and theological understanding to the interpretation of his experiences of mental illness. It is necessary to understand the core values and meanings contained in the ministry of incarnation in the setting of an apocalyptic eschatological setting. I will thus reflect on Boisen's *living human document* in the light of apocalyptic thinking in a modern context.

1. ANTON THEOPHILUS BOISEN AND HIS LIVING HUMAN DOCUMENT

Anton Theophilus Boisen (1876–1965) was the instigator of the clinical pastoral education movement which he developed through his own experiences when he suffered a mental breakdown. From his experience of the care given by specialists he felt that their pastoral practice bore little relationship to the experience of the Christian seeking help. Hence he developed a theory called the *living human document* in 1925.[1] This theory grew into the practice known as clinical pastoral education (CPE). In order to analyze this concrete data of human experience, a *verbatim report*, that is, a word-for-word recording method, was needed.[2] The clinical pastoral movement developed its own discipline of pastoral theology in the early twentieth century.

Charles Gerkin summarized many of Boisen's concepts in his book *The Living Human Document*. He claims that Boisen's comments can be reduced to four major points: he wishes for open-minded discussion, no categorization, hearing on its own merit (the patient's in-depth life experience), and respecting the patient's in-depth life experience which is to be revered on the same level as the historic texts which the Judeo-Christian faith are based.[3]

Seward Hiltner in his journal article "The Heritage of Anton T. Boisen" asserts that Boisen was influenced by the theological liberalism of the early twentieth century and that Albert Schweitzer and George A. Coe (Boisen's teacher) had a particularly strong impact upon Boisen.[4] However, Boisen had a diverse range of theological views and was not interested in one particular stream of theology and as a result theologians struggled to categorise him in his time. Nevertheless, the theory he espoused, or the *living human document*[5] became influential.

Robert David Leas commented that the revelation of Boisen's theological experience was the discovery of the potential for power within powerlessness, the very meaning of the crucifixion-resurrection event in Christian theology.[6] Leas quotes from John Patton's lecture that Boisen's theological legacy "came from the power of relationship to reach out and affirm the humanness of the separated ones—those trapped in loneliness,

---

1. Boisen, *Exploration of the Inner Word*, 9–10. See Boisen, "The Challenge to Our Seminaries," 12, Gerkin, *Living Human Document*, 200 (chapter 2, footnote 1), and Nouwen, "Anton T. Boisen," 59.
2. Leach, *Pastoral Supervision*, 268.
3. Gerkin, *Living Human Document*, 38.
4. Hiltner, "Heritage of Anton T. Boisen," 5–10.
5. Hiltner, "Heritage of Anton T. Boisen," 6.
6. Leas, *Anton Theophilus Boisen*, 190.

confusion and powerlessness."[7] For Boisen, this was starting to bring together the kingdom of God and social issues in a way not seen since the early part of the twentieth century. However, this was not simply a return to the social gospel. It was something new which offers fresh insights for apocalyptic perspectives for our time.

2. MESSIANIC CONSCIOUSNESS AND SCHWEITZER'S ESCHATOLOGICAL VIEW ON BOISEN'S THEOLOGY

Christians have always linked apocalyptic imagery and the vision of the kingdom of God. From the Greek word *apokalypsis*—the revelation of something hidden, this genre of literature gets its name *apocalyptic*. Christians spoke of a ghastly and violent climax to the contemporary phase of world history, in which the order would dissolve into fire and out of which a new divine order would emerge. It was during the late nineteenth and early twentieth centuries that apocalyptic and eschatological perspectives were rediscovered as a very significant part of the kingdom of God.

Johannes Weiss, in *Jesus' Proclamation of the Kingdom of God*, at the turn of the twentieth century, declared Wolfgang Ritsch's view of the kingdom of God to be unbiblical and warned that the apocalyptic teaching of Jesus was being ignored.[8] Weiss went back to the New Testament and examined it in its first-century setting. By applying the apocalyptic outlook to the teachings of Jesus, Weiss had reintroduced eschatological thinking into the church and emphasized the lordship of God in controlling the end of the age.

Albert Schweitzer took it further and applied the apocalyptic outlook not only on the teachings of Jesus but to the New Testament as a whole, in his book *The Quest of the Historical Jesus*. He used the Synoptics and Q (Quelle) sources in order to retrace the path of the liberal researchers for the historical Jesus and utilized the same materials with an eschatological outlook. In his book, Schweitzer claimed that the attempt to get at the life of Jesus was an attempt to bring Jesus into the present. However, we cannot understand the historical Jesus from the classical-liberal viewpoint of Schweitzer's time which saw the kingdom as ethical in nature. Schweitzer said, "But He does not say; He passes by our time and returns to His own.

---

7. Leas, *Anton Theophilus Boisen*, 190. See Patton, *Dicks-Boisen Lecture*, May 10, 2006.

8. Moltmann, *Theology of Hope*, 38.

What surprised and dismayed the theology of the last forty years was that, despite all forced and arbitrary interpretations, it could not keep Him in our time, but had to let Him go. He returned to His own time."[9] It can be seen that at the beginning of the twentieth-century apocalyptic and eschatological perspectives had been rediscovered as a very significant part of the kingdom of God.

In chapter 4 of his book *The Exploration of the Inner World*,[10] Boisen explored Jesus' messianic consciousness and asked the question, "What did Jesus think of himself?" Interestingly Boisen adopted the eschatological view of Schweitzer. Eschatology has become an important theme in theology since the exegetical works of Weiss and Schweitzer at the beginning of the twentieth century. Boisen claimed that Jesus held both messianic and eschatological ideas, which Schweitzer also believed.[11]

Boisen wrote of the messianic consciousness of Jesus within the Marcan sources, Harnak's Q sources, and Luke. Boisen pointed out, through numerous references to eschatology in his book,[12] the important role of Jesus in proclaiming this good news of the kingdom of God and self-awareness of his fate.[13] For Boisen, all sources of the Gospels were a witness to Jesus as messiah since it "represented him as teaching his disciples clearly and explicitly that he was to die, and making their own willingness to die for the sake of the kingdom a condition of discipleship."[14] Boisen concurs with Schweitzer's eschatology that these references have a "distinctly apocalyptic"[15] outlook in character and confirms the eschatology of Jesus.

Although Christians have always linked apocalyptic imagery and the vision of the kingdom of God, Ulrich H. J. Körtner commented that it was through the contributions of Weiss and Schweitzer that apocalyptic thought came into the consciousness of theology.[16] Jürgen Moltmann in *Theology of Hope* writes that Schweitzer's contributions to apocalyptic

---

9. Schweitzer, *Quest of the Historical Jesus*, 396.
10. Boisen, *Exploration of Inner Word*, 125–41, and Boisen, *Out of the Depths*, 194–96.
11. Boisen, *Exploration of Inner Word*, 132.
12. Boisen, *Exploration of Inner Word*, 132–35.
13. Boisen, *Exploration of Inner Word*, 133.
14. Boisen, *Exploration of Inner Word*, 132–33.
15. Boisen, *Exploration of Inner Word*, 133.
16. Körtner, *End of the World*, 8.

thinking have been of great value for modern theology and that apocalyptic vision provides hope to people.[17]

In the light of Schweitzer's view, Boisen noted that Jesus "held both the messianic and the eschatological ideas."[18] Schweitzer concludes that "He will reveal Himself in the toils, the conflicts, the sufferings which they shall pass through in His fellowship, and, as an ineffable mystery, they shall learn in their own experience Who He is."[19]

For Boisen, Jesus looked upon his death as essential to the accomplishment of his mission, and he expected his resurrection.[20] Boisen believed that within the historical Jesus, the kingdom of God has already arrived through his teachings, but a new world (kingdom of God) will come immediately after an "imminent world catastrophe"[21] This view of the *already* and *not yet* represents apocalyptic thinking and for Boisen embodies Schweitzer's *ineffable mystery*. Boisen believed that "Jesus did think of himself as the Messiah"[22] and that "he looked forward to a messianic parousia."[23] I will discuss further the place of apocalyptic thinking in terms of theology.

3. APOCALYPTIC THINKING AND THEOLOGY

Apocalyptic Thinking in Terms of Theology

In the previous section, I mentioned the word apocalyptic being derived from the Greek *apokalypsis*—an uncovering. To expand further, Norman Perrin describes "a movement in Judaism and Christianity that characteristically claimed that God had revealed to the writer the secrets of the imminent end of the world and so had given him a message for his people."[24] He claimed that an explanation of the terms *apocalyptic* and *eschatology* (from the Greek *eschatos*—the end of things) is in order. In considering the world

---

17. Moltmann, *Theology of Hope*, 38.
18. Boisen, *Exploration of Inner Word*, 132.
19. Schweitzer, *Quest of the Historical Jesus*, 401.
20. Boisen, *Exploration of Inner Word*, 134.
21. Boisen, *Exploration of Inner Word*, 132.
22. Boisen, *Exploration of Inner Word*, 130.
23. Boisen, *Exploration of Inner Word*, 130.
24. Perrin, *Apocalyptic Christianity*, cited in Hanson, *Visionaries*, 121.

of the New Testament, *apocalyptic* is a particular form of *eschatology*.²⁵ Therefore apocalyptic is a specific type of eschatology, not its alternative.²⁶

John J. Collins goes further and defined in his book *The Apocalyptic Imagination*:

> An apocalypse is a genre of revelatory literature with a narrative framework, in which a revelation is mediated by an otherworldly being to a human recipient, disclosing a transcendent reality which is both temporal, insofar as it envisages eschatological salvation, and spatial insofar as it involves another, supernatural world.²⁷

The content of the apocalypse presents in the form of a prophecy, the culmination in a time of crisis and eschatological upheaval.²⁸ We understand Collins's view that the apocalyptic perspective determined Jesus' life in the New Testament. In the temporal sense Jesus was the historical Jesus in the eschatological event and in the spatial sense Jesus died and was resurrected and will come again.

Collins comments in his theological implication at the end of his book that "the legacy of the apocalypses includes a powerful rhetoric for denouncing the deficiencies of this world. Most of all it entails an appreciation of the great resource that lies in the human imagination to construct a symbolic world where the integrity of values can be maintained in the face of social and political powerlessness and even of the threat of death."²⁹

In his book *A New Heaven and a New Earth*, J. Richard Middleton states the word *apocalypse* means the "unveiling or disclosing of the hidden that occurs with God in the world and history."³⁰ Middleton clarified an important pattern that frames New Testament eschatology. The New Testament anticipates that creation will be redeemed, but we do not presently see all things redeemed. Therefore he sees that the tension is not between sin and redemption, but rather between partial and complete redemption, with the partial (in heaven) being a guarantee of full salvation to come (on earth).

The eschatological pattern is the coming of Jesus fulfilled (already—partial), whereas the apocalypse pattern is waiting for the coming of Jesus

25. Perrin, *Apocalyptic Christianity*, in Hanson, *Visionaries*, 121.
26. Körtner, *End of the World*, 51.
27. Collins, *Apocalyptic Imagination*, 4.
28. Collins, *Apocalyptic Imagination*, 5.
29. Collins, *Apocalyptic Imagination*, 215.
30. Middleton, *New Heaven*, 152.

(not yet).³¹ He said that the apocalyptic pattern is dependent on the "temporal sequence of Christ's incarnation, ascension, and second coming—Parousia."³² The hoped-for restoration of all things is still in the future.

Regarding Parousia, Middleton particularly interprets 1 Thess 4:13–18 with the image of the second coming of Jesus and his celebration. In the context of the Roman Empire, celebrating the incarnation of Jesus, as the king of kings, was not feasible. It was only about something to reflect on for the future, in the hope that that day will come. It would be a great event and announced with great fanfare, and with his coming, the Lord will judge the world and make all things new.³³

The incarnation of Jesus is already the beginning of the new world. Importantly, the hope of the incarnation of Jesus is to bring hope, justice, peace, and reconciliation, and although these are still here on Earth, they have not been completely fulfilled, but remain in everyone's hope. This was disclosed through the death and resurrection of Jesus, but is still yet to be completely fulfilled. It is expected with an apocalyptic hope with the depiction of the new heaven and the new earth (Rev 21:1–8). Middleton said that this apocalyptic pattern is clearly dependent on the temporal sequence of Christ's incarnation, ascension, and second coming, or parousia.³⁴

Ernst Käsemann affirmed in his essay "The Beginnings of Christian Theology" that "Apocalyptic was the mother of all Christian theology. Historically, apocalyptic ideas played an important role in early Christianity"³⁵ He further discussed in his book *New Testament Questions of Today* the subject of primitive Christian apocalyptic. He researched Pauline theology regarding Paul's understanding of the righteousness of God (see Rom 5:17; 1 Cor 1:30; 2 Cor 5:21; Gal 3:6) and stated that Paul interpreted this in an apocalyptic setting from a perspective of universalism. Käsemann claimed that Bultmann's interpretation of Pauline theology from an anthropological viewpoint reduces its universalism to the justification of the individual.³⁶

---

31. Middleton, *New Heaven*, 213.
32. Middleton, *New Heaven*, 213.
33. Middleton, *New Heaven*, 222–23.
34. Middleton, *New Heaven*, 213.
35. Käsemann, "Beginning of Christian Theology," 17–46.
36. Käsemann, *New Testament Questions*, 15.

Rather, Paul understood "God's action in Christ as in the creation of the world"[37] under the sense of apocalyptic influence.[38]

R. Dean Drayton, in his book *Apocalyptic Good News*, researched the apocalyptic emphasis showing the apocalyptic in Paul's experience on the Damascus road. He states apocalypse is a divine event that "unexpectedly beyond expectation and knowledge happens to a person or group."[39] An apocalyptic unveiling is a radical historical event where God appears within space and time, as well as during times of crisis and danger for his people, so as to save and offer hope to society. Drayton said that "in the life, death, resurrection, and ascension of Jesus, an apocalypse has already happened. It is an irruption into space and time that lets space and time be seen in new ways."[40] He said "this redemption in Christ Jesus is available for all. It is the apocalyptic reality."[41]

Drayton explored J. Louis Martyn's commentary in Galatians about Paul meeting the resurrected Jesus on the road to Damascus. Martyn interpreted Paul's Damascus road event as the apocalyptic event in which God appears within space and time.[42] For Paul, the apocalypse is the breaking in upon the reality of the resurrected Jesus Christ, disclosing the way that the God of Jesus Christ is at work in the midst of creation and history.[43] As a result of his experience, Paul's witness is pivotal in shaping the mission of the early church and the growth of the Gentile church in the empire.[44]

Moltmann begins his book *Theology of Hope* with a discussion about eschatology. This is based largely on the perspective of hope represented by Bloch.[45] Moltmann interpreted hope with God's promise in the Exodus event.

The God of hope revealed in Exodus is disclosed in the crucified and resurrected Christ, who identified his suffering with human suffering in the world. Moltmann stated that "Christian eschatology in the language of

---

37. Käsemann, *New Testament Questions*, 181.
38. Käsemann, *New Testament Questions*, 181.
39. Drayton, *Apocalyptic Good News*, 32.
40. Drayton, *Apocalyptic Good News*, 32.
41. Drayton, *Apocalyptic Good News*, 29.
42. Drayton, *Apocalyptic Good News*, 30–31, 37.
43. Drayton, *Apocalyptic Good News*, 33.
44. Drayton, *Apocalyptic Good News*, 138.
45. Moltmann, *Theology of Hope*, 16.

promise will . . . be an essential key to the unlocking of Christian truth."[46] Moltmann includes catastrophe in the apocalypse. The death of Jesus Christ is a catastrophe. How could the Messiah, the son of God, die? Although he was resurrected and appeared to his disciples, the death of Jesus was still a catastrophe for his disciples. However, "with Christ's resurrection from the catastrophe of Golgotha the new beginning has already been made, a beginning which will never again pass away because it issues from the victory over transience."[47]

Moltmann comments on the concept of today's phrase *apocalypse now* as distinct from apocalyptic traditions of hope, and that today, we are concerned about self-made apocalypses in which there is no hope. Examples could include nuclear war, ecological, biological or natural disasters. Consequently, these are end-times without hope. However the Christian tradition of apocalypse is the bringing of hope in times of danger.[48] Moltmann writes that "Apocalypse is the message of hope in danger, and encouragement to see the danger clearly and to resist hopelessness of a self-made apocalypse."[49] Moltmann said the crucified Jesus identifies with all people who are in sadness, suffering, injustice, and fear within the world.[50]

Moltmann asserts that apocalyptic thought has a cosmological view. He concluded that apocalyptic thought seeks to understand eschatology connecting to cosmology. He said that "without apocalyptic a theological eschatology remains bogged down in the ethnic history of men or the existential history of the individual. The New Testament did not close the window which apocalyptic had opened for it towards the wide vistas of the cosmos and beyond the limitations of the given cosmic reality."[51] Throughout history the apocalyptic movement has arisen among the oppressed people of the world. Jesus aimed to teach and prepare his disciples to live in this world as well as telling them to look for the new age. It helps us to see that Christianity is a religion which at its heart offers hope.[52]

---

46. Moltmann, *Theology of Hope*, 41.
47. Moltmann, *In the End*, 48.
48. Moltmann, *In the End*, 48–50.
49. Moltmann, *In the End*, 51.
50. Moltmann, *Crucified God*, 29.
51. Moltmann, *Theology of Hope*, 137–38.
52. Lee, *Religion and Social Formation*, 19.

Apocalyptic Thinking from a Social Aspect

Apocalyptic thinking is concerned with social practice in the sense of the wider society. Such thinking relates to a widespread desire for radical change by those who face injustice, oppression or persecution. The early Christian community waited for the kingdom of God on Earth, waiting for the relief Jesus Christ would bring from evil; a new world, a new order.[53] This is important as it shows us that "Christianity was not merely a spiritual movement, but also a social movement."[54]

However, the early Hellenistic ideology changed the political and social circumstances to an individual and beyond-world concept.[55] Collins said in his book *The Apocalyptic Imagination* that "the affinities of the apocalypses with widespread Hellenistic conception can be seen by considering two clusters of texts, the first involving otherworldly journeys.... This classical tradition is marked by strong philosophical interests, which are quite different from what we find in the Jewish apocalypses."[56]

Boisen reflected on the evangelical groups and their message. They claimed that "man's nature is regarded as innately bad and a new birth is necessary for salvation."[57] Boisen notes that "this salvation, while not without a strong ethical content, is thought of largely in other-worldly terms"[58] and laments that their intense focus on "saving souls" made them "lose sight of the relationship of these souls to a public order."[59]

Boisen saw and recognized the sick and suffering society,[60] where the mentally ill were isolated, marginalized, ignored, and vulnerable. He said that "many society evils are tolerated because their implications in terms of concrete human suffering go unnoticed. Our culture has thus become mechanized and depersonalised."[61] The kingdom of God welcomes these people, and as Jesus had welcomed these people, Boisen saw that society needed to welcome these people. That is a healthy society. In an apocalyptic

---

53. Lee, *Religion and Social Formation*, 19.
54. Lee, *Religion and Social Formation*, 19.
55. Collins, *Apocalyptic Imagination*, 26–28.
56. Collins, *Apocalyptic Imagination*, 26.
57. Boisen, *Exploration of Inner World*, 85.
58. Boisen, *Exploration of Inner World*, 85.
59. Boisen, *Religion in Crisis and Custom*, 128.
60. Boisen, *Religion in Crisis and Custom*, 9.
61. Boisen, *Religion in Crisis and Custom*, 131.

setting, the oppressed people waited for a messiah who brought power within powerlessness and hoped for the day of liberation from bondage. Boisen found out two directions of inwardly human being and his social responsibility from the messianic Jesus, and claimed the two are harmonized in Jesus. Boisen said that "the significance of Jesus would then lie precisely in the fact that with a true sense of the social responsibility which rested upon him he achieved also the highest degree of harmony, not only inwardly but in his social perspective."[62]

How does apocalyptic thinking connect with the incarnation of Jesus? Apocalyptic thinking and its tradition leads us to meet the incarnation of Jesus who came to the world as the son of God, and the incarnation of Jesus is the center. We will continue to explore how the incarnation of Jesus can be linked to CPE.

4. INCARNATION OF JESUS AND APOCALYPTIC THINKING

Understanding Jesus within Apocalyptic Thinking

Howard Clark Kee, in his book *Community of the New Age: Studies in Mark's Gospel*, researched the Gospel of Mark and related the apocalyptic outlook to social and cultural issues so as to understand the community setting of Mark.[63]

In Jesus' time his ministry was exercised among the sick, the outcasts, and the demon-possessed (Mark 1:32–34; 5:7–13; 6:7–13). In Mark 1:24, the demon addresses Jesus as "the holy one of God." Kee researched that this term appeared in the apocalyptic tradition of the book of Daniel (Dan 7:18, 22, 25) and the book of 1 Enoch (1 En 14:1) where God is called "the Holy One," that is, the one which foretells the defeat of the demonic powers.[64] Mark assigned this title to Jesus in the demonic miracle narratives as the one who is the victor over demonic rule.[65] Kee claimed that "redemption is not seen by Mark as extrication from a hostile context in which man lives, but as renewal and ordering of that context, exemplified by these cosmic powers he described working through Jesus."[66]

---

62. Boisen, *Exploration of the Inner World*, 139.
63. Kee, *Community of the New Age*, 13.
64. Kee, *Community of the New Age*, 34–35.
65. Kee, *Community of the New Age*, 120.
66. Kee, *Community of the New Age*, 121.

So Mark discussed the issues of Sabbath, ritual purity, divorce and women's rights, obligation to secular authority, attitudes toward possessions, moral responsibility to one's neighbor, love for one's neighbor, watchfulness, and prayer, with Mark's portrayal of Jesus.[67] Mark's Gospel presents Jesus as the one who interprets the will of God to God's new people. Jesus prepared his disciples to live in this world as well as telling them to look for the new age—an apocalyptic vision.

Elizabeth Shively discussed this story of the demon in her book *Apocalyptic Imagination in the Gospel of Mark*. Mark 5:1–20 is the longest miraculous narrative where Jesus struggled to set free the oppressed from Satan's power in order to create a new community.[68] Briefly, "Jesus encounters a man *from the tombs* with an *unclean spirit* in the area of the *Gerasenes* whose gentile orientation and uncleanness is illustrated by the presence of a herd of swine."[69]

Mark evokes the "apocalyptic symbolic world" to interpret Jesus' ministry as a skirmish in a dualistic cosmic contest in which the Spirit-empowered Jesus wages war against Satan to rescue people held captive by demonic powers.[70] Mark depicted Jesus as the holy One of God,[71] the Son of God, who judges over the power of evil and heals the unclean man in an apocalyptic setting.[72]

In Mark 5:6–7, when the unclean man saw Jesus from afar, he ran to him, worshipped him and cried with a loud voice, "What do you want with me, Jesus, Son of the Most High God? In God's name don't torture me!" He cried in agony, begging Jesus not to torture him and asking him to swear by God. Mark knew that the God of Exodus was the God who heard the cries of people in slavery and remembered his covenant with Abraham, Isaac, and Jacob (Exod 2:23–24).

The kingdom of God proclaimed by Jesus welcomes everyone. In Mark's Gospel, Jesus welcomed the sick, lepers, those who were taken by demons, tax collectors, Gentiles, and the socially marginalized, who were called sinners. Mark reports that Jesus has authority as the son of man to forgive sins and can resist the power of evil. We can compare the exorcism

67. Kee, *Community of the New Age*, 118, see also 151–62.
68. Shively, *Apocalyptic*, 172.
69. Guelich, *Mark*, 283.
70. Shively, *Apocalyptic*, 175.
71. Kee, *Community*, 35.
72. Shively, *Apocalyptic*, 173.

of the *Gerasene* demoniac in the Gospel of Mark with the Gospel of Matthew and the Gospel of Luke. Matthew's version in 8:1—9:34 falls within a section that highlights Jesus' healing ministry. He shortens the story but interprets this great power with Jesus casting out spirits and healing diseases, as fulfilling Isaiah's prophecy: "He took our illnesses and bore our diseases" (Matt 8:17).[73] Luke's perspective held that Jesus identifies with the suffering messiah to share man's suffering in the world (Luke 8:26–39).[74]

In comparison, for Mark, this story is a battle between Jesus and the kingdom of Satan.[75] Thus, Shively comments that the Gerasene Demoniac in Mark 5:1–20 is a recontextualization of apocalyptic thinking: persecution, interference of heavenly beings, and judgment[76] and states that "this story demonstrates that Jesus' defeat of the evil spirits amounts to a defeat of the power of death. As a result, the man experiences restored life and the blessing of community."[77]

Therefore this apocalyptic story in Mark's narrative is significant. That is, Jesus as the Holy One and as the key figure in Mark's community inaugurates the new age. In the new age his kingdom makes a place for the socially marginalized, the outcasts, those who in the world are the most unimportant people, and even the unclean people.

Derek Tidball comments in his book *An Introduction to the Sociology of the New Testament* that sickness, enforced loneliness or demonic possession are only signs of the total grip that evil had on the society in Jesus' time. Hence Jesus explained his mission by identifying himself with those who desired change.[78]

In the Old Testament, the prophets prioritized justice for poor people rather than ritual sacrifice. When Robert Wilson researched prophetic tradition in his book *Prophecy and Society in Ancient Israel*, prophetic tradition articulated the people's longing and hopes.[79]

Isaiah claims that God really wants the flourishing of humanity, embodied in the healing of the social order and of those who are suffering.[80]

---

73. Shively, *Apocalyptic*, 176.
74. Shively, *Apocalyptic*, 176.
75. Shively, *Apocalyptic*, 177.
76. Shively, *Apocalyptic*, 183.
77. Shively, *Apocalyptic*, 183.
78. Tidball, *Sociology of the New Testament*, 31.
79. Wilson, *Prophecy and Society*, 292.
80. Middleton, *New Heaven and a New Earth*, 104.

It means that when the Jewish liturgy of sacrifices, Sabbaths, and festivals demonstrate God's compassion and justice toward others, the nature of worship will be recognized by God (Isa 58:1–14). As Middleton comments on Isa 58:6, "The logic of the prophetic critique is that although worship is an explicit claim of allegiance to YHWH, such a claim must be backed up with justice, which is a concrete demonstration of this allegiance."[81]

In his book *Kingdom and Community*, John G. Gager points out that Jesus' activities in the gospels reflect a perfect image of the millenarian (apocalyptic) prophet, for he combines criticism of the old with a vision of the new,[82] since "not only must he comprehend the present crisis and proclaim the promise of a new order, he must in some sense embody that order in the present."[83]

Luke described Jesus as someone who identified himself as a prophet (Luke 4:24; 7:16; 13:33; 24:19). Jesus declaimed his own ministry by proclaiming good news to the poor, release for captives, recovery of sight to the blind and setting at liberty the oppressed. Jesus read out the prophetic promise of Isaiah at the synagogue in his hometown of Nazareth:

> The Spirit of the Lord is upon Me, Because He has anointed Me
>
> To preach the gospel to the poor; He has sent Me to heal the brokenhearted,
>
> To proclaim liberty to the captives And recovery of sight to the blind,
>
> To set at liberty those who are oppressed; To proclaim the acceptable year of the Lord. (Isa 61:1–2; Luke 4:18–21)

In the Gospel of Matthew, Jesus linked the prophets with the Moses tradition in his teaching of the greatest commandment (Deut 6:5; Lev 19:18) regarding love of God with love of neighbor. Jesus revealed the God of the exodus in his teaching and ministry. Jesus said, "Do not think that I came to destroy the Law or the Prophets. I did not come to destroy but to fulfill" (Matt 5:17). Jesus affirms that ministry actions are regarded as expressing service linked to a life of justice, mercy, and faithfulness. This is taught through the parable of the sheep and the goats at the end of Days. God judged nations on the basis of their actions of compassion toward those in need (Matt 25:31–46). This is the apocalyptic prophetic tradition,

---

81. Middleton, *New Heaven and a New Earth*, 104.
82. Gager, *Kingdom and Community*, 29.
83. Gager, *Kingdom and Community*, 32.

which Jesus practices. The vulnerable people of the world waited for the return of their king who they hoped would fulfill their hopes and dreams. When Jesus as the king came he understood their needs but he issued a final judgment. The king will reply, "Truly I tell you, whatever you did for one of the least of these brothers and sisters of mine, you did for me" (Matt 25:40). When you cared for others, you cared for me. When you visited others, you visited me. This apocalyptic practice embodied the spiritual and social action of Jesus for his people—the socially, physically, and spiritually deprived people of the world, and pastoral carers should aim to practice this edict.

In John's book of Revelation, the expectation of the apocalypse, and the new heaven and new earth begins with Jesus in the midst of creation and history (Rev 22), where God heals the wounded creation, saying, "He will wipe every tear from their eyes. There will be no more death or mourning or crying or pain, for the old order of things has passed away. He who was seated on the throne said, 'I am making everything new!' Then he said, 'Write this down, for these words are trustworthy and true'" (Rev 21:4–5).

The vision of the new heaven and the new earth shows God's grace of forgiveness, healing, reconciliation, and sanctification disclosing God's love through Jesus' ministry in his death and resurrection. We can say that the identity of an apocalyptic vision can be fulfilled by the incarnation of Jesus who reveals God's love and his compassion of salvation for the world. The incarnation of Jesus was a fulfillment of God's promise to save humankind and to restore all creation. We will continue to explore how the meaning of the incarnation of Jesus can be linked to CPE.

Christlike Ministry and the Living Human Document as a Social Biography

Boisen was mortally afraid of mental illness because he was affected by this problem. In his era the average citizen had little understanding of mental illness and so they treated mentally ill people very cruelly and harshly. Influenced by his experience, Boisen formed a different outlook, saying "mental illness is the price we have to pay for being men and having the power of choice and the capacity for growth."[84]

Boisen studied Paul's experience on the road to Damascus and particularly noted the Roman governor's remark, who upon hearing Paul's witness, shouted, "You are out of your mind, Paul! Your great learning is

---

84. Boisen, *Out of the Depths*, 196–97.

driving you insane" (Acts 26:24). For Boisen, "that remark [had] a familiar ring,"[85] as Paul and the men of his time would not for a moment deny that there was a certain relationship between his experience and those of the insane. From this deeply personal experience of mental illness, Boisen commented that "certain types of mental disorders and certain types of religious experiences were attempts at reorganisation,"[86] that is, the "operation of the healing forces of nature."[87]

In his autobiography, Boisen recalls the mental breakdown he suffered in 1920, when he was forty-four years of age. He wrote of being taken away to a hospital by six policemen at the request of his family and his description of his stay seemed to feel like a thousand years to him.[88]

Although it was a horrifying tragedy for him, he also wrote that his experience as a mental hospital patient was "a clear-cut conversion experience, with effects which were wholly beneficial"[89] and allowed him the opportunity to open his new work regarding the living human document. Henri Nouwen commented in his article "Anton T. Boisen and Theology through Living Human Documents" as follows:

> His experiences are the essential ingredients of his new approach to theology: the study of living human document and Boisen himself is the first human document that asks for careful study.... Boisen was 44 years old when he entered the hospital and he brought to the disturbed period a great wealth of experiences, thoughts, and feelings which were grounded in his illness and model into a life project. It grows into the practice known as Clinical Pastoral Education (CPE).[90]

Religion in Crisis and Custom was written by Boisen in 1945, twenty years after he developed his concept of the living human document. It is a "sociological and psychological study of religion with special reference to American Protestantism"[91] in which he provides the basis of action in CPE. Boisen suggests that the "emphasis upon the rights of the individual, to be

---

85. Boisen, *Exploration of Inner World*, 58.
86. Boisen, *Exploration of Inner World*, viii.
87. Boisen, *Exploration of Inner World*, viii.
88. Boisen, *Out of the Depths*, 86–87.
89. Boisen, *Out of the Depths*, 138.
90. Nouwen, "Anton T. Boisen," 52.
91. Boisen, foreword to *Religion*.

socially valid, must be supplemented by a corresponding emphasis upon the individual's responsibility for the common good."[92]

Boisen is critical of overarching individualism such as private interest, private salvation, self-centeredness, and the lack of concern for others. He suggests that individual rights ought to be accompanied by the "individual responsibility for the common good."[93] Boisen also considers the individual as "part of a social organism."[94] For Boisen the personal and social are interdependent. He comments on the social concern of Jesus:

> The significance of Jesus would then lie precisely in the fact that with a true sense of the social responsibility which rested upon him he achieved also the highest degree of harmony, not only inwardly but in his social perspective. This we explain by the view that here was a man who brought to the crisis experience no mere concern about his personal destiny.[95]

Boisen's criticism of supreme individualism is not limited to the secular world. For instance, he notes the lack of concern in striving for improved social and economic conditions of the underprivileged by the Pentecostal sects that ironically often arise from such settings.[96] He continues:

> There is nothing in their message which goes to the heart of the problems of this sick and suffering world. They are content to let it get worse and worse. They have no social vision, no promise of salvation beyond that which is to come miraculously when the Lord returns in glory.[97]

Boisen wrote of the expectation of the apocalypse, of the *new Jerusalem*, the *new heaven and the new earth* that is made possible with Jesus in the midst of creation and history as expressed in Revelation 22.[98] Boisen sees that the vision of the new Jerusalem in John's book of Revelation is different from the vision of Christendom. He claimed that Christendom today is torn with

---

92. Boisen, *Religion*, 252.
93. Boisen, *Religion*, 252.
94. Boisen, *Exploration*, 139.
95. Boisen, *Exploration*, 139.
96. Boisen, *Religion*, 91.
97. Boisen, *Religion*, 91.
98. Boisen, *Exploration*, 289.

war and hatred between nations and between classes and there is grave danger that it may destroy itself.[99]

Boisen did not agree with the view of his time that religion is an "escape from reality."[100] He said that religious concern should be associated with awareness of danger and with attempts to face personal difficulties.[101] Boisen recognized the limitation of religion as a cult which escapes from this world and he knew the dangers of Christendom as the dominant form that remained in this world.

Boisen's experience is an example of a *living human document*. It demonstrates the ability to connect personal experiences, and social and theological understanding to interpreting his problems. Clients face many social problems. These include political, economic, social justice, reconciliation, ethnic conflict, refugees, gender discrimination, and women's rights issues.

Boisen's *living human document* focuses on human beings rather than books or doctrine. In other words, theology is not a means to itself, but it is for people. If a person can be seen as a living document, then it records the sickness, hardship, and trauma of that suffering person. In this light we should take Boisen's *living human document* from a wide-ranging perspective because people are influenced by the cultural, social, political, and economic contexts they are in. As an examination of an apocaltic thinking, clinical pastoral education must be prophetic in denouncing the structures of evil and encountering the kingdom of oppression. CPE should help people to meet the incarnation of Jesus to set them free from their captivity so that they may have joy, happiness, and hope for their future.

Therefore, apocalyptic thinking requires a reflection on both the *living human document* and the *social biography*[102] of the troubled person, so that they may find a new heaven and new earth. In other words, it is the discovery

---

99. Boisen, *Exploration*, 180.
100. Boisen, *Exploration*, 212.
101. Boisen, *Exploration*, 212.
102. The term "social biography" was utilized by Korean Minjung theologians. Yong Bok Kim mentioned millennial hope. That is, while the Korean people were under the oppressive rule of Japan, "the Coming Messiah," "the New Heaven," "the New Earth," and "the New Jerusalem" in the book of Revelation could be seen as a historical reference of the experiences of the Korean people. His understanding of the Messiah was someone who identifies with the suffering people. In the context of Korean history, the experiences of the oppressed were historical and collective (Kim, *Minjung Theology*, 109). Nam Dong Suh (Korean Minjung Theologian) saw this experience as the "social biography of the minjung [oppressed Koreans]" (Kim, *Minjung Theology*, 157).

of joy, happiness, and a new way forward, in the same way as the people who walked on the road to Emmaus were touched by the apocalyptic Jesus who is the incarnated and resurrected Jesus. Hence, the importance of the concept that apocalyptic thinking is an eschatological future that is universal and open to all, beyond the "limitations of the given cosmic reality" and the "existential history of the individual."[103]

Alan Galt, who is the director of the Mental Health Clinical Pastoral Education Centre, has said that CPE is based on a *Christlike ministry*,[104] that is, the incarnation of Jesus and for him, CPE is also open to ministry with people from other faiths. Thus, CPE is open to diversity in a multicultural context. He has developed a theological reflective model of CPE. For Galt theological reflection is not the means of developing a theology. Rather, theological reflection involves the search for the person who is suffering through listening with empathy and God's compassion, and allows the patient to speak openly about their worries and concerns without fear of being judged, dismissed or ignored.[105]

God's love is the presence of God for those who are in the midst of their losses, disappointments, and uncertainties. God is the God who is listening to their crying and who is sending us to them as his agent in order to share God's love with them in secular society.[106] God's love revealed in Christ is not only for Christians, but for the whole world, including the secular. God, who was revealed in Christ and the history of Israel, is now revealed to all humankind. This is a social and spiritual reaction revealing God's compassion. Galt states in his biblical reference (Matt 25: 31–46), "When you visited others, you were visiting me." This means that carers become involved with CPE which is based on a Christlike ministry in a secular society.

5. PASTORAL REFLECTION ON GOD'S LOVE: AN APOCALYPTIC LOVE AND ALICE IN BOISEN'S STORY

Another significant factor in influencing Boisen's thought was his love for Alice Batchelder. Boisen's autobiography, *Out of the Depths*, is centered on his great love of Alice. In 1902, Boisen (twenty-six years old) met and fell in

103. Moltmann, *Theology of Hope*, 137.
104. Galt, see ch. 1 of this book.
105. Alan Galt's lecture, September 2019.
106. Alan Galt's lecture, September 2019.

love with Alice Batchelder (twenty-five years old). They did not marry, but remained friends for thirty-three years until in 1935 when Boisen learned that Alice was dying of cancer and she passed away the same year. Boisen writes:

> On August 24, 1935, I received a note from Alice, saying that she was going into retirement for an operation and that the edict had gone forth—No callers, no flowers. I discovered soon that the difficulty was cancer and that the outlook was hopeless.[107]

Boisen expressed his feelings as follows:

> I began to see things from her standpoint. How often I had disappointed her! What poor use I had made of our friendship, failing in these later years to reach the deeper levels of understanding![108]

His expression *I began to see things from her standpoint* suggests Boisen realizes that when we imagine ourselves in the standpoint of others we can understand that person and when we cannot do this, we do not understand that person. In *Out of the Depths*, Boisen discovers the need to see things from the standpoint of others in order to find the underlying meaning of their suffering and their unique history and problems. It seems apparent that the journey of the *living human document* for Boisen relates to God's love revealed in Jesus' death and resurrection. He described God's love as a father's love. He said that "belief in the fatherhood of God . . . is rooted in the love which is the deepest need of the human."[109]

Boisen's love for Alice was not romantic, sexual, or secular in nature. For him, this love was a symbol of light, an angel, a "bridge over every chasm"[110] and it represents the enduring hope of all those suffering from mental illness. Boisen's love for Alice Batchelder is a metaphor for God's love in his life and in his mind. The role of love is to comfort, to strengthen and to help the capacity for growth. As well as giving encouragement, Boisen also believed that this love can care for those who are in need.

Boisen describes Alice more like a guardian angel rather than a woman of this world, just as Beatrice was for Dante. He said, "I was at once interested, for ever since my decision not to give up hope in my love for

---

107. Boisen, *Out of the Depths*, 176.
108. Boisen, *Out of the Depths*, 174.
109. Boisen, *Religion in Crisis and Custom*, 199.
110. Boisen, *Exploration of the Inner Word*, dedication page.

Alice, Dante had been for me a sort of patron saint, and I had kept his picture hanging in my room."[111]

In his autobiography, Boisen writes about Alice:

> In all that I have done she has been an indispensable factor, and hers the harder and more difficult role. She had to suffer for my mistakes and slowness of mind. She was a rarely gifted woman who, on my account, never found her highest usefulness.... Her compassion for me, her wisdom, her courage, and her unswerving fidelity have made possible the measure of success I have achieved.[112]

We need to understand Dante's *The Divine Comedy* in order to appreciate the expression of Boisen's feelings for Alice. Dante Alighieri (ca. 1265–1321) was a powerful political leader in his time until losing his position and lived in exile. It was during this time that he started to write *Divine Comedy*. It is a narrative in which the protagonist Dante journeys through hell, purgatory, and paradise or heaven, guided by two beings. His narrative is a thoroughly apocalyptic work within the tradition of the apocalyptic imagination. It was written in 1301, during the period of his exile in Florence.

Virgil, the ancient Roman poet who greatly influenced and was admired by Dante, arrives at the gates of hell, where it is written:

> Nothing till I was made was made, only
> eternal beings. And I endure eternally.
> Surrender as you enter every hope you have.[113]

Dante comments on the meaning of hell by describing it as a place where there is no hope, where neither sun nor stars can be seen. He navigates hell with Virgil, travels through purgatory and eventually arrives in paradise. He is now able to see the sky and the light, and sense hope. At this point, Beatrice appears. She welcomes Dante and guides him through paradise.

In his life, Dante met Beatrice when they were nine years old. He was instantly besotted with her and maintained a deep love for her until they met again nine years later, where he saw her passing by with a friend, Lady Vanna, along the Arno River. Upon seeing Dante, Beatrice greeted him which filled his heart with great joy. Although they never married, Dante

---

111. Boisen, *Out of the Depths*, 154.
112. Boisen, *Out of the Depths*, 210, see final chapter.
113. Dante, *Divine Comedy: Inferno*, canto 3, 7–9. See Boisen, *Exploration*, 15.

never forgot her and for him, she was a powerful living symbol of love and hope, acting as a guide in his life.

In *The Divine Comedy*, Virgil leaves Dante in the hands of Beatrice who guides him through heaven. Beatrice is a reflection of Dante's love whom he meets again in heaven, a place of love where hope is recovered. Beatrice is Dante's love recovered, heaven is described through the stars and God is within the bright light that shines upon all. In essence, for Dante heaven is love, hope, and light:

> See! Beatrice with so many saints
> closes her hands in prayers along with mine . . .
> All powers of high imagining here failed.
> But now my will and my desire were turned,
> as wheels that move in equilibrium,
> by love that moves the sun and other stars.[114]

For Boisen, Alice was his love, hope, and light. In the midst of his darkness, she gave him strength, comfort, and spiritual guidance. The meeting of Alice is to provide a hopeful future in the relationship between them. It is an exodus for Boisen, allowing him to journey out of his darkness. For him it is the *living human document* that contains hope, love, and promise. His love for Alice was an apocalyptic love that allowed him to escape darkness, despair, and sadness, and find a new energy and renewal for his life. At the end of Boisen's autobiography we can read of his apocalyptic power of love for Alice:

> I am thinking of the old Dante-Beatrice story, in which the poet had to pass through the fire before he could enter Paradise and join the woman he worshiped . . . a man's love for a woman is such that he draws not from the common source of strength, but clings to her, that man is not worthy of her. It was necessary for me to pass through the purgatorial fires of a horrifying psychosis before I could set foot in my promised land of creative activity.[115]

For Boisen, apocalyptic love is a love found beyond a couple's *common source of strength*. It is a love that supports those who are clinging onto life with hope and promise. Boisen describes his own love of Alice as a love in

---

114. Dante, *Divine Comedy: Inferno*, canto 33, 37–39, 142–45.
115. Boisen, *Out of the Depths*, 207–8.

which an unworthy man clings onto a woman,[116] but was nevertheless a "guiding hand" for him.[117]

For Boisen, his love for Alice—this *guiding hand*—strengthened his resolve to defeat the power of his darkness—mental illness—and it accompanied his whole life through the darkness of purgatory. The memory of Alice helped Boisen's own case to develop the *living human document*. Boisen echoed his love for Alice with God's love through apocalyptic imagery and metaphors that Dante described. Boisen's concern here is pastoral rather than the theological speculative and therefore, the mystery of the love of God for us in the crucified and resurrected Christ, lies at the heart of Boisen's assurance and the grounds of pastoral work.

Boisen comments on how love is integral to our existence, characterized by the *idea of God*, and states that the idea of God is a symbol of the deep need and longing for people to be with those whom they love and with those whom they owe their allegiance. This is regarded as enduring and universal in society.[118] For Boisen, this love is always within us, and is the basis of life and acts as our guidance in life because "the structure of society is based on love."[119]

Through his whole life, Boisen's experience of love, faith, and his mental illness were resources in the development of the *living human document*. In his Statement of Confession, Boisen wrote, "I believe in love which came to my rescue on that Easter morning long years ago . . . this love is one with the God."[120] Boisen believed that "God was once perfectly revealed in the life, character, and teachings of Jesus of Nazareth"[121] and that "the deepest desire of every human heart is that for love."[122]

---

116. Boisen, *Out of the Depths*, 208.

117. Boisen, *Out of the Depths*, 209. De Bono notes in *Exploration and Adaptation* that Boisen's love of Alice moved from a finite to an infinite relationship (162). See also Nouwen, "Anton T. Boisen," 57, and Boisen, *Out of the Depths*, 197.

118. Boisen, *Exploration of Inner Word*, 196.

119. Boisen, *Exploration of Inner Word*, 197.

120. Boisen, *Exploration of Inner Word*, 296.

121. Boisen, *Exploration of Inner Word*, 296.

122. Boisen, *Exploration of Inner Word*, 289–90.

CONCLUSION

I have discussed how apocalyptic thinking could be thought of as a way of bringing new hope to society in the context of oppression or despair in relation to the practice of clinical pastoral education.

Boisen's concern was the connection between pastoral theology and the client's situation and experience. In order to analyze this *concrete data of human experience*, Boisen asserted, "I have sought to begin not with the ready-made formulations contained in books but with the living human documents and with actual social conditions in all their complexity."[123] This statement suggests how beliefs and practice or ministry and life should connect with each other, so that the Christian identity may be expressed in the secular world.

For this discussion of apocalyptic thinking, I explored Boisen's resources that display his understanding of Schweitzer's eschatological viewpoint and that a reference to Schweitzer would be sufficient evidence to present an argument that relates to the incarnational Jesus. I discussed the modern theologian's idea of an apocalyptic thinking that Jesus was the incarnation of the Messiah. Therefore, not only can the *living human document* be seen as a personal living document, it can also be seen as a social biography from an apocalyptic perspective.

CPE is a practice which draws on and participates in the love of God through the incarnation of Jesus in the world. In addition, it also explores the love between Alice and Boisen, comparing it with an apocalyptic lover in Dante's apocalyptic story. I believe Boisen's own cases of mental illness, on which he based his first *living human document*, was a biblical reflection through apocalyptic thinking. He showed us the possibility of linking personal experience, social identity, and theological understanding to the interpretation of his experiences of mental illness.

The practice of CPE is valuable to individuals, but it is also a social practice where it can be reflected on in terms of an apocalyptic thinking. It is a program which goes to hospitals and nursing homes. It is a social program that encompasses all marginalized people and those suffering from injustice. CPE is not being blind to worldly issues. CPE must go into refugee camps, children's orphanages, and migrant camps. CPE must seek those suffering injustice, those under oppressive regimes, and those who suffer from abuse. CPE practitioners may be drawn not only to care for

---

123. Boisen, *Exploration of Inner World*, 185.

individuals and families, but to actively participate in efforts to transform society due to God's ministry in the secular world. As Jesus once said, "I needed clothes and you clothed me, I was sick and you looked after me, I was in prison and you came to visit me" (Matt 25:36). This is CPE—the concern for both the spiritual and social life of others as well as the concern of God through a *Christlike ministry*.

God's love is the basis of pastoral work in the context of human suffering, pain, and death. Apocalyptic vision is connected to hope for those who are suffering oppression, poverty, injustice, and the many conflicts of society. Apocalyptic thinking may act to embrace the people who are broken and wounded, spiritually, socially, and politically.

CPE is not simply caring for private and personal vulnerabilities. It is the showing of a vision to the vulnerable in society and the revealing of God's true justice within dehumanization. It is showing reconciliation from division between people and people, nation and nation. These are the showing of the incarnational ministry of Jesus which is his crucifixion, resurrection, ascension, and coming again.

Apocalyptic thinking predicates a new social order coming into what may become the new heaven and the new earth. CPE practitioners will journey to look forward to seeing the new heaven and new earth, and the good news in order to make a new kind of society and to heal the sick society for the people of the world. We will see the opening of a new possibility of Boisen's *living human document* as a *social biography* when we act for the people with *apocalyptic thinking*, which is the presence of God that is already here, through the action of clinical pastoral education in the secular world.

BIBLIOGRAPHY

Anderson, Ray S. *The Shape of Practical Theology: Empowering Ministry with Theological Praxis*. Downers Grove: InterVarsity, 2001.

Arbuckle, Gerald A. *Culture, Inculturation, and Theologians: A Postmodern Critique*. Collegeville: Liturgical, 1996.

Bauckham, Richard. *New Testament Theology: The Theology of the Book of Revelation*. Cambridge: Cambridge University Press, 1993.

Bevans, Stephen B. *Models of Contextual Theology*. New York: Orbis, 2002.

Biziou, Barbara. *The Joy of Ritual*. New York: Cosimo, 1999.

Boisen, Anton T. "The Challenge to Our Seminaries." *Journal of Pastoral Care* 5 (1951) 8–12.

———. *The Exploration of the Inner World*. New York: Willett, Clark, 1936.

———. *Out of the Depths: An Autobiographical Study of Mental Disorder and Religious Experience*. New York: Harper, 1960.
———. *Problems in Religion and Life: A Manual for Pastors*. New York: Abingdon-Cokesbury, 1946.
———. *Religion in Crisis and Custom: A Sociological and Psychological Study*. New York: Harper, 1955.
Bosch, David J. *Transforming Mission: Paradigm Shifts in Theology of Mission*. Maryknoll: Orbis, 2017.
Brueggemann, Walter. *An Introduction to the Old Testament*. Louisville: Westminster John Knox, 2003.
Buttrick, George Arthur, ed. *The Interpreter's Bible—New Testament Articles, Matthew and Mark*. Vol. 7. Nashville: Abingdon, 1952.
Case, Shirley Jackson. *The Millennial Hope*. Chicago: University of Chicago Press, 1918.
Chupungco, Anscar J., ed. *Handbook for Liturgical Studies: Introduction to the Liturgy*. Vol. 1. Collegeville: Liturgical, 1997.
Collins, John J. *The Apocalyptic Imagination: An Introduction to the Jewish Matrix of Christianity*. New York: Crossroad, 1987.
Congar, Yves. *At the Heart of Christian Worship*. Translated by Paul Philibert. Collegeville: Order of Saint Benedict, 2010.
Dante, Alighieri. *The Divine Comedy*. Translated by Robin Kirkpatrick. London: Penguin, 2012.
De Bono, Christopher E. "An Exploration and Adaptation of Anton T. Boisen's Notion of the Psychiatric Chaplain in Responding to Current Issues in Clinical Chaplaincy." PhD diss., University of St. Michael's College, 2012.
Drayton, R. Dean. *Apocalyptic Good News: Christ in the Cosmos*. Eugene, OR: Resource, 2019.
Dunn, James D. G. *Romans 1–8*. World Biblical Commentary. Dallas: Word, 1988.
Egan, Gerard. *The Skilled Helper: A Systematic Approach to Effective Helping*. 7th ed. Belmont: Brooks/Cole, 2002.
Erickson, Millard J. *Contemporary Options in Eschatology*. Grand Rapids: Baker, 1977.
Gager, G. John. *Kingdom and Community*. New Jersey: Prentice Hall, 1975.
Gelder, Craig Van, and Dwight J. Zscheile. *The Missional Church in Perspective: Mapping Trends and Shaping the Conversation*. Grand Rapids: Baker Academic, 2011.
Gerkin, Charles V. *The Living Human Document: Re-visiting Pastoral Counselling in a Hermeneutical Mode*. Nashville: Abingdon, 1984.
Goheen, Michael W. *Introducing Christian Mission Today: Scripture, History and Issues*. Downers Grove: InterVarsity, 2014.
Guder, Darrell L. *The Continuing Conversion of the Church*. Grand Rapids: Eerdmans, 2000.
Guelich, Robert A. *Mark 1—8:26*. World Biblical Commentary. Dallas: Word, 1989.
Hanson, Paul D, ed. *Visionaries and Their Apocalypses*. London: SPCK, 1983.
Hawn, C. Michael. *One Bread, One Body: Exploring Cultural Diversity in Worship*. Herndon: Alban Institute, 2003.
Hennecke, Edgar. *New Testament Apocrypha*. Vol. 2, *Writings Relating to the Apostles Apocalypses and Related Subjects*. Edited by Wilhelm Schneemelcher. Translated by R. McL. Wilson. Philadelphia: Westminster, 1965.
Hewson, Daphne, and Michael Carroll. *Reflective Practice in Supervision*. Hazelbrook, Australia: MoshPit, 2016.

Hiltner, Seward. "The Heritage of Anton T. Boisen." *Pastoral Psychology*, November 1965, 5–10.
Howard, Barbara. "Touching Christ's Wounds: 25th Anniversary of Women's Priesting." 2017. http://newcastleanglican.org.au/wp-content/uploads/2018/01/Touching-Christs-wounds.pdf.
Hughes, Graham. *Worship as Meaning: A Liturgical Theology for Late Modernity*. Cambridge: Cambridge University, 2003.
Hunsinger, Deborah Van Deusen, and Theresa F Latini. *Transforming Church Conflict: Compassionate Leadership in Action*. Louisville: Westminster John Knox, 2013.
Käsemann, Ernst. "The Beginning of Christian Theology." *Journal for Theology and Church* 6 (1969) 17–46.
———. *New Testament Questions of Today*. London: SCM Press, 1969.
Kee, Howard Clark. *Community of the New Age: Studies in Mark's Gospel*. Macon, GA: Mercer University Press, 1983.
Kim, Young Bock, ed. *Minjung Theology*. Singapore: Commission on Theological Concern, 1981.
Körtner, Ulrich H. J. *The End of the World: A Theological Interpretation*. Louisville: Westminster John Knox, 1995.
Kreminski, Karina. *Urban Spirituality: Embodying God's Mission in the Neighborhood*. Skyforest: Urban Loft, 2018.
Leach, Jane, and Michael Paterson. *Pastoral Supervision: A Handbook*. 2nd ed. London: SCM Press, 2015.
Leas, Robert David. *Anton Theophilus Boisen: His Life, Work, Impact, and Theological Legacy*. Journal of Pastoral Care Publications, 2009.
Lee, Sang Taek. *The Kingdom of God in Korea*. Seoul: Yang Suh, 1988.
———. *Religion and Social Formation in Korea: Minjung and Millenarianism*. Berlin: Mouton de Gruyter, 1996.
MacKinlay, Elizabeth. *The Spiritual Dimension of Aging*. London: Kingsley, 2001.
McKnight, Scot. *A Community Called Atonement*. Nashville: Abingdon, 2007.
Middleton, J. Richard. *A New Heaven and a New Earth: Reclaiming Biblical Eschatology*. Grand Rapids: Baker Academic, 2014.
Moltmann, Jürgen. *The Crucified God*. Minneapolis: Fortress, 2015.
———. *In the End—the Beginning: The Life of Hope*. Minneapolis: Fortress, 2004.
———. *Theology of Hope*. New York: SCM Press, 1967.
Moynagh, Michael. *Church for Every Context: An Introduction to Theology and Practice*. London: SCP Press, 2012.
Nouwen, Henri J. "Anton T. Boisen and Theology through Living Human Documents." *Pastoral Psychology*, September 1968, 49–63.
———. *The Living Reminder: Service and Prayer in Memory of Jesus*. New York: Seabury, 1977.
Nussbaum, Stan. *A Reader's Guide to Transforming Mission*. Maryknoll: Orbis, 2005.
Perrin, Norman. *The New Testament: An Introduction*. New York: Harcourt Brace Jovanovich, 1974.
Powell, Peter. *Story Whispering: An Introduction to Biblical-Narrative Therapy*. North Parramatta, Australia: Pastoral Counselling Institute, 2014.
Saliers, Don E. *Worship as Theology*. Nashville: Abingdon, 1994.

Schweitzer, Albert. *The Quest of the Historical Jesus: A Critical Study of Its Progress from Reimarus to Wrede.* 3rd ed. Translated by William Montgomery. London: Black, 1954.

Sharpe, Eric J. "The Kingdom, the Power and Glory." Unpublished paper, Department of Religious Studies, University of Sydney.

Shively, Elizabeth E. *Apocalyptic Imagination in the Gospel of Mark: The Literary and Theological Role of Mark 3:22–30.* Edited by James D. G. Dunn and Carl Holladay. Berlin: de Gruyter, 2012.

Tanner, Kathryn. *Theories of Culture.* Minneapolis: Augsburg Fortress, 1997.

Thompson, Judith, et al. *SCM Studyguide to Theological Reflection.* London: SCM Press, 2008.

Tidball, Derek. *An Introduction to the Sociology of the New Testament.* Exeter: Paternoster, 1983.

Wilson, Robert R. *Prophecy and Society in Ancient Israel.* Philadelphia: Fortress, 1980.

Woodward, James, and Stephen Pattison, eds. *The Blackwell Reader in Pastoral and Practical Theology.* Malden: Blackwell, 2000.

Notes on the Contributors

Rev. Alan Galt, OAM, center director and CPE education consultant, has been a Uniting Church Minister since 1966. He studied psychology and anthropology at Sydney University, theology at the Methodist Theological College and Melbourne College of Divinity, and has an MA in counseling from Macquarie University. He was awarded a Churchill Fellowship to study community development in Israel to assist his work with integrating Outback indigenous communities. A mental health chaplain for thirty-five years; and a CPE supervisor for forty years; he has been secretary of the NSW Council (now College) for CPE; convenor of its accreditation subcommittee; and academic dean. He is a senior lecturer in pastoral theology with the Sydney College of Divinity; runs education and supervision in pastoral ministry for people from all faith traditions; and works with members of Korean and Orthodox churches to facilitate the effectiveness of their pastoral ministry.

Rev. Dr. Peter Walker, principal of the United Theological College since 2019, was assistant director of the Public and Contextual Theology Research Centre at Charles Sturt University and acting director of the Australian Centre for Christianity and Culture. He studied history, philosophy, and theology at the University of NSW, McGill University, and Charles Sturt University and has served as a visiting fellow at Dunmore Lang College, chairperson of United Theological College Council, chairperson of the Presbytery of Canberra Region, president of the Australian Capital Territory Council of Churches, and is currently a board member and assistant editor of the *International Journal of Public Theology*. At Charles Sturt School of Theology he teaches subjects in the history of Christianity, with particular research interest in Christianity in early Modern Europe, and Christian-Muslim engagement.

Notes on the Contributors

Ms. Jennifer Washington is the pastoral care manager at St Vincent's Hospital, Sydney, after working as a CPE supervisor/educator at the hospital from 1996 to 2015. She has been involved in the formation of CPE supervisors since 2005. Trained as a primary school teacher, she also has a BTh, MCounseling, and an MA (specialization in pastoral supervision). She first entered a CPE program at Royal North Shore Hospital, Sydney, in 1987. Jenny is a past president of the NSW College of CPE and also of the Australian and New Zealand Association of CPE Supervisors, and as the academic dean of the NSW CPE College, guides the college's planning for its educational and supervision activities in the rapidly changing environment of twenty-first-century Australia. She has been central in promoting clinical pastoral education in the Catholic colleges, hospitals, and parishes, and through the Sydney College of Divinity to the people from its other member institutions.

Rev. Prof. Rodney Dean Drayton is an adjunct research professor of the Centre for Christianity and Culture within Charles Sturt University and a minister of the Uniting Church, having worked extensively in the practice and teaching of mission and evangelism and pastoral ministry. A geophysicist ordained in the "Death of God" era, he was executive director of the Board of Mission in the Synod of New South Wales for sixteen years, moderator of the New South Wales Synod of the Uniting Church (1995–1996); national president of the Uniting Church in Australia (2003–2006). He is the author of *Pilgrim in the Cosmos* (1995), *Which Gospel?* (2005), and *Apocalyptic Good News* (2019). Dean was a visiting professor in evangelism at the Southern Methodist University's Perkins School of Theology in Dallas, Texas. In 1999, he was appointed lecturer in theology (missiology and evangelism) at the United Theological College in Sydney.

Rev. Dr. Peter Powell is a Uniting Church in Australia minister, a teacher with the Sydney College of Divinity, a registered psychologist with clinical accreditation (adults) in the NSW Child Sex Offender Counsellors Accreditation Scheme, clinical member, Australian and New Zealand Association for the Treatment of Sexual Abusers. Peter is a provisional educational consultant with the NSW College of Clinical Pastoral Education. He graduated from the Illinois Pastoral Services Institute (three-year psychotherapy residency) and Garrett-Evangelical Theological Seminary, Illinois (doctoral degree in pastoral counseling and psychotherapy) with a dissertation on "Cross-Gender Friendships: Implications for the Marital Dyad." He is the author of books on a biblical approach to behavior change and therapy and has presented numerous papers and conducted training seminars on educational and behavioral strategies with difficult children, and the treatment of men committing sex offences against children. Peter is past president of the NSW College of Clinical Pastoral Education and runs introductory CPE programs for indigenous communities in rural NSW and in the Pacific Islands.

Rev. Morris Sing Key is a NSW Presbyterian minister who has been for two decades the main provider of CPE courses for NSW conservative denominations. A provisional CPE education consultant, he has been president of the NSW CPE College and a central part of our planning to retain people from all NSW churches in the CPE movement. Morris has devised the approach that individual CPE centers and CPE supervisors could decide whether to include people from other faiths in their pastoral education and supervision programs or not. Until recently he has been the director of the Westmead CPE Centre, and he was engaged by the church in Indonesia to promote CPE there. Morris teaches in the Morling Baptist College Pastoral Theology program, including a wide range of pastoral theology and clinical pastoral education activities.

Mrs. Heather Robinson is the executive secretary of the NSW College of CPE, a provisional CPE educator, and a supervisor with the Mental Health CPE Centre. She has supervised introductory and basic programs for the Iona Korean College and the Cumberland Mental Health CPE Unit, which is being offered partly by distance learning during the pandemic lockdown. A mother and grandmother, Heather has also been chair of her church council and a part-time chaplain with the Macquarie Psychiatric Hospital pastoral care team. She is an advocate for the Blue Knot Foundation, whose purpose is "the affording of relief, assistance and support to diseased, disabled, sick, infirm, incurable, poor, destitute, helpless, or unemployed persons, or to the dependents of any such persons," and has a special interest and expertise in ministry with people affected by the "complex trauma" of childhood abuse.

Mrs. Rosemarie Say, OAM, is an associate teacher with the Sydney College of Divinity, CPE educator and mental health chaplain. While training as a psychiatric nurse, Rosemarie was awarded the gold medal as top student. When her children started school, she worked as a volunteer for over twenty years, mainly in child abuse prevention and grief support services, and when her children left home, she launched a new career in mental health

CPE, graduating with an MA (pastoral supervision) in 2010. In 2015 she was awarded a Medal of the Order of Australia (OAM) "For service to community health, particularly mental health services." Now, working full time, pursuing her passion in mental health chaplaincy, she conducts training as a CPE educator in this increasingly vital area. In her spare time, she cherishes happy times with her husband, David ("the wind beneath my wings"), and a delightful extended family of four children and eight grandchildren, declaring, "I have had a blessed life!"

Rev. Dr. Sang Taek Lee, OAM, is a minister of the Uniting Church in Australia, and a former adjunct lecturer of the United Theological College, the School of Theology, Charles Sturt University. He is currently the principal and CEO of Iona Columba College, Sydney, Australia. Sang Taek received his PhD from the University of Sydney and was awarded an Order of Australia Medal (OAM) for services to the community. He is the author of a number of books, including *New Church New Land* (Uniting Press, Melbourne), and *Religion and Social Formation in Korea: Minjung and Millennial Hope* (Mouton de Gruyter, Berlin/New York) as well as being known for his long-standing work in ministry, spirituality, and theology. He has sought to pass on his enthusiasm of CPE to the Korean community in Australia and is currently a provisional CPE supervisor.

Index

A
Action-Reflection model, 10, 63, 79, 91
apocalyptic, 48–49, 105–21, 123–30
    catastrophe, 110, 114
    eschatology, 108–11
    love, 124, 127, 129
    millenarian, 119
    millennial hope, 105, 123
    thinking, 105–6, 115–16, 118, 123–24, 129–30

B
Batchelder, Alice, 124–29
Black fella, 67
Boisen, Anton T., 9, 15–16, 92–93, 101, 105–10, 115–16, 120–130
boundary, 40–41, 45, 59

C
Christendom, 122–23
Christlike, 9, 83, 124
Clinebell, Howard, 8, 95, 98
Collins, John J., 111, 115
Council for CPE, 3
creativity, 28–30, 33
cultural identity, 62, 64

D
Damascus, 48, 113, 120
Dante, Alighieri, 125–29
De Certeau, Michel, 20
Divine Comedy, 126–27
Drayton, R. Dean, 113

F
Fitchett, George, 70

G
Galt, Alan, 82, 88, 124
Gerkin, Charles V., 107
grace, 47–48, 50, 52–53

H
Harnak, 109
healing, 44–45, 52, 121
Hellenistic ideology, 115
Helping Style Inventory, 36
Hickin, Marlene, 84
Hiltner, Seward, 72, 107
Holifield, E. Brooks, 40

I
incarnation, 112, 116, 120, 123–24

J
Jarvis, Peter, 34–35, 37
Johnstone, Colin B., 76

K
Käsemann, Ernst, 112–13
Kee, Howard Clark, 116–17
Kelly, Ewan, 99–100
Körtner, Ulrich H. J., 109, 111

L
language, 58–62
Lartey, Emmanuel Y., 72
Leas, Robert David, 107–8

living human document, 17, 107, 121, 123, 125, 127–30
living human web, 17

M
Mental Health CPE unit, 6
Middleton, J. Richard, 111–12, 118–19
Minjung, 123
Moltmann, Jürgen, 108–10, 113–14
multi-faith, 41, 100
multicultural, 6, 41, 124

N
Nicholas of Cusa, 17–25
Nietzsche, Friedrich, 92
Nouwen, Henri J., 85, 92, 121

O
other faiths, 6–7, 11, 41

P
predominant cultures, 41
presence of God, 12, 124, 130

R
Rogers, Carl, 95

Rohr, Richard, 96

S
Schleiermacher, Friedrich, 15
Schrage, Michael, 29
Schweitzer, Albert, 107–10, 129
Shively, Elizabeth, 117–18
social biography, 123, 129–30
social practice, 115, 129
St Augustine, 8

T
Theological Reflection template, 88
Tidball, Derek, 118

V
VanKatwyk, Peter L., 36
vision of God, 20–21, 23
Volf, Miroslav, 27–28, 34

W
Wagner, Willard, 96
Weiss, Johannes, 108–9
Western religion, 44
White fella, 58, 62–64, 67

www.ingramcontent.com/pod-product-compliance
Lightning Source LLC
Chambersburg PA
CBHW072143160426
43197CB00012B/2231